EDITOR: LEE JOHNSON

OSPREY
MILITARY

NEW VANGUARD

KV-1&2
HEAVY TANKS 1939-1945

Text by
STEVEN ZALOGA & JIM KINNEAR
Colour plates by
PETER SARSON

First published in Great Britain in 1995 by
Osprey Publishing, Elms Court, Chapel Way, Botley,
Oxford OX2 9LP, United Kingdom.
Email: info@ospreypublishing.com

ISBN 1 85532 496 2

Edited by Iain MacGregor
Page design: the Black Spot
Filmset in Great Britain
Printed in China through World Print Ltd.

FOR A CATALOGUE OF ALL BOOKS PUBLISHED BY
OSPREY MILITAR AND AVIATION PLEASE CONTACT:

The Marketing Manager, Osprey Direct UK,
PO Box 140, Wellingborough, Northants,
NN8 4ZA, United Kingdom.
Email: info@ospreydirect.co.uk

The Marketing Manager, Osprey Direct USA,
c/o Motorbooks International, PO Box 1, Osceola,
WI 54020-0001, USA.
Email: info@ospreydirectusa.com

VISIT OSPREY AT
www.ospreypublishing.com

Author's Note

The authors would like to thank many friends for help in
preparing this book. First and foremost to the noted
armour expert Janusz Magnuski's, whose pioneering work
on the history of Soviet tanks made this book possible.
Thanks also to Stephen 'Cookie' Sewell for help with
many Russian articles. Several friends in Russia were kind
enough to provide excellent new archival photos from their
collections, including Andrey Aksenov, Aleksander
Koshchavtsev, Rustem Ismagilov and Slava Shpakovskiy.
Finally, the authors would like to thank the staff of the
Kubinka armour museum for their assistance. Where possible, the authors have attempted to credit the Soviet combat photographers whose photos appear in this book.

Artist's Note

Readers may care to note the original paintings from which
the colour plates in this book were prepared are available
for private sale. All reproduction copyright whatsoever is
retained by the Publishers. All enquiries should be
addressed to:

Peter Sarson
46 Robert-Loius Stevenson Avenue
Westbourne
Bournemouth
BH4 8EJ

The Publishers regret that they can enter into no corre-
spondence upon this matter.

Editor's note

Readers may wish to read this title in conjunction with the
following Osprey titles:

KV-1&2 HEAVY TANKS 1939-1945

DESIGN AND DEVELOPMENT

After the First World War, several European armies toyed with the idea of a heavy tank to assist in breakthrough operations. The first of these was the French Char 2C, but it was followed by others such as Britain's Independent. These were aptly dubbed 'land battleships', bristling with several turrets and gun stations. The Red Army became infatuated with the concept, but was not able to act until the early 1930s, when Stalin's industrialisation drive made the series production of such heavy tanks feasible. From 1932 to 1939, a total of 61 T-35 heavy tanks were manufactured at the Kharkov Locomotive Factory. By the end of the 1930s, it was obvious that the T-35 was obsolete. But the Red Army was firmly wedded to the dramatic appeal of the multi-turreted land battleship. One unrealistic scheme was the redesign of the T-35 design into the 95 ton T-39, fitted with three turrets with a 152 mm howitzer, 107 mm gun and 45 mm gun. There

was little confidence that such a heavy design could be built or that it would be practical in combat and the project never left the drawing board.

Pre-war tank design theories

The experience of Soviet tankers in the Spanish Civil War made it clear that tanks would have to survive anti-tank guns of 37 mm calibre or greater, and the emphasis in heavy tank design shifted from heavy firepower to heavier armour.

In 1937 the Main Directorate of the Armoured and Mechanised Forces (GABTU), solicited proposals for an 'Anti-tank Gun Destroyer' with 'shell-proof' armour able to withstand the fire of 37-45 mm anti-tank guns at point-blank range, or the fire of 75 mm field guns at 1200 metres. The new programme was deemed important enough that two design bureaus in Leningrad were assigned to develop competitive prototypes, the N. Barykov bureau at the Bolshevik Factory and the new Special Design Bureau 2 (SKB-2), headed by Zhozef Kotin at the Kirovskiy Plant.

The original requirement called for the same layout as the T-35, ie, five turrets. The engineers quickly convinced GABTU to eliminate the 'decorative' MG

The first of the Soviet multi-turreted heavy tanks was the T-35, seen here in its standard production form during a parade in Moscow in the 1930s. Although the idea of multiple gun turrets looked good on paper, in practice, they proved impractical.

The proto-types of the new generation heavy tanks were sent to Finland for combat trials at the end of 1939. This is the Barykov design bureau's T-100 'Sotka' heavy tank in operation in Finland. The T-100 proved overweight and underpowered in combat, due in part to its archaic multi-turreted configuration.

turrets, reducing the requirement to three turrets: the main turret with a 76 mm gun, and two smaller turrets with 45 mm anti-tank guns. The Barykov team called their design the T-100, or *Sotka* – Russian slang for '100'. The Kotin team followed the current Leningrad fad for naming everything after the murdered communist party boss Sergei M. Kirov – hence 'SMK'. Both design teams began to work on 'sketch projects' of their proposed designs.

The original version of the SMK used the same antiquated type of suspension as the T-35, but this was later deemed too heavy. As an alternative, the design team tested a new torsion bar suspension on a modified T-28 medium tank and this was adopted on the SMK. On 4 May 1938, wooden models of the designs were shown to a special meeting of the State Defence Council (GKO) in Moscow. Kotin questioned the utility of three turrets, which prompted Stalin to approach one of the wooden models, break off one of the turrets and quip: 'Why make a tank into a department store!' The meeting confirmed the decision to use 60 mm armour on the new tanks in spite of the formidable manufacturing problems this presented.

The KV and T-100 projects

The May 1938 meeting led to the redesign of both the

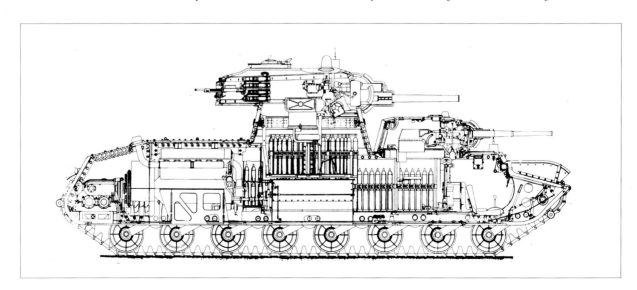

Kirovskiy Plant Cross-sectional Drawing of the SMK Heavy Tank.

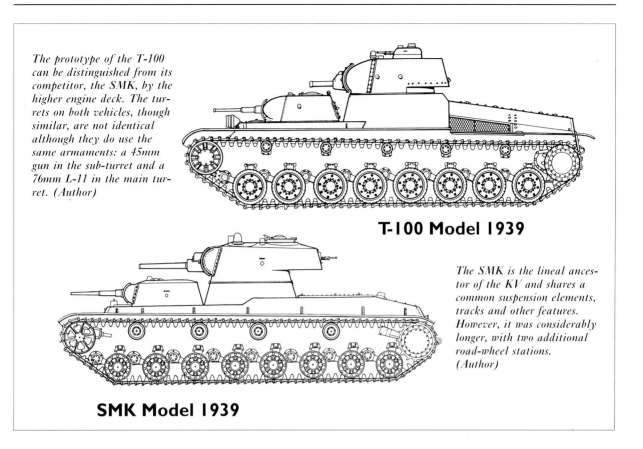

The prototype of the T-100 can be distinguished from its competitor, the SMK, by the higher engine deck. The turrets on both vehicles, though similar, are not identical although they do use the same armaments: a 45mm gun in the sub-turret and a 76mm L-11 in the main turret. (Author)

T-100 Model 1939

SMK Model 1939

The SMK is the lineal ancestor of the KV and shares a common suspension elements, tracks and other features. However, it was considerably longer, with two additional road-wheel stations. (Author)

SMK and T-100 projects. The Kotin design team became convinced that a more practical approach would be to eliminate the second 45 mm gun turret as well, and simply use a single 76 mm gun turret. The problem with the twin-turret design was that it inevitably forced the designers to mount the main turret on a large, heavily armoured pedestal. This added considerable weight to the design, which could better be used as thicker armour on a single-turret version. The projected single-turret tank was named 'KV' after Stalin's crony, Marshal Klimenti Voroshilov, the People's Defence Commissar, who also happened to be Kotin's father-in-law. The KV design effort at SKB-2 was headed by N.L. Dukhov, while the SMK effort was headed by A.S. Yermolayev. In August 1938, the Central Committee of the Communist Party held a meeting to discuss the future of tank production, and the revised designs of the SMK and T-100 were shown to Stalin. Kotin also displayed his projected KV design. Although not based on a GABTU requirement, Stalin approved construction of prototypes of the KV as well as the SMK and T-100.

Two T-100 prototypes were built, each weighing about 58 tonness and crewed by seven men. There were two turrets, the uppermost armed with a short L-11 76.2 mm gun and the lower with a 45 mm Model 1938. The L-11 was a new 76.2 mm tank gun,

The last survivor of the 1939 heavy tank project is this SU-130 'Igrek' SP gun, currently preserved at the Kubinka armour museum near Moscow. This vehicle was built on the chassis of one of the two T-100 heavy tanks. Although the SU-130 did not enter production, this prototype was used in the defence of Moscow in 1941.

The war in Finland convinced the Red Army of the need for a heavy howitzer tank to destroy bunkers. A small number of KV hulls were modified with a special large turret, fitted with a 152 mm howitzer, later called the KV-2. This early production KV-2 of the 5th Tank Division was abandoned in its entrenchment near Alitus, Lithuania, during Operation 'Barbarossa' in June 1941. (US National Archives)

AM-34 aero engine. The KV was significantly smaller than either the SMK or T-100 and was powered by a Trashutin V-2 diesel engine, the same as used in the T-34 medium tank. The KV prototypes had the advantage of being 8 tons lighter than the SMK, as well as having thicker armour. Trials of all three designs began in September 1939 at the state proving grounds at Kubinka, and were attended by a special state acceptance commission headed by Marshal Voroshilov. The trials indicated that the T-100, 3 tonnes over the 55 tonne limit, was sluggish and difficult to drive. In the case of both the T-100 and SMK, the commander had difficulty co-ordinating the actions of both gun turrets,

The first series production batch of KV-1 tanks, sometimes called the KV-1 Model 1939, had the L-11 76 mm gun. This weapon, developed by the SKB-4 at the Kirovskiy Plant, did not meet with official approval, and was quickly replaced by the F-32 gun designed by the Grabin artillery design bureau.

designed by the Machanov team of the SKB-4 artillery design bureau of the Kirovskiy Plant as a replacement for the L-10 76.2 mm gun used on the T-28 medium tank and T-35 heavy tank. It not only armed all of the heavy tank prototypes, but the new T-34 prototype as well. The SMK prototype was a similar configuration to the T-100 with the same armament arrangement. Both the T-100 and SMK were powered by GAM-34-8T petrol engines, a 850 hp version of the Mikulin

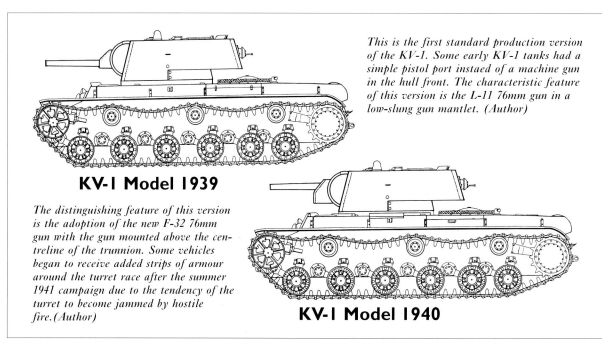

KV-1 Model 1939

This is the first standard production version of the KV-1. Some early KV-1 tanks had a simple pistol port instaed of a machine gun in the hull front. The characteristic feature of this version is the L-11 76mm gun in a low-slung gun mantlet. (Author)

The distinguishing feature of this version is the adoption of the new F-32 76mm gun with the gun mounted above the centreline of the trunnion. Some vehicles began to receive added strips of armour around the turret race after the summer 1941 campaign due to the tendency of the turret to become jammed by hostile fire. (Author)

KV-1 Model 1940

The standard production variant of the KV-2 used a new turret design, using a simpler curved side panel. This vehicle was captured by the Wehrmacht in 1941 and sent back to Germany for trials. It was back in use in 1945 at Krupp's Essen plant in an ill-fated attempt to defend the facility against advancing US troops.

a not altogether surprising result since the T-35 was notorious for the same shortcoming. The KV quickly emerged as the best of the three designs.

Setbacks in Finland

While the trials at Kubinka continued, the Red Army was involved in its botched invasion of Finland. The small but fiesty Finnish army had handed the cumbersome and poorly led Red Army a series of bloody defeats. The performance of the Red Army's tank force was particularly embarrassing. Some of the problems were due to the design features of the tanks; as had been the case in Spain, they were pervious to 37 mm anti-tank guns. As a result, a special company of the 20th Armoured Brigade was formed under Major P. Voroshilov, son of the Defence Commissar, and equipped with the new heavy tank prototypes. Manned in part by factory crews, they were used in the assault on the Finnish 'Velikan' bunker complex around Summa, where they they had some initial successes against the poorly armed Finns. However, the SMK drove over a large mine which blew off one of its tracks and buckled the belly armour. The remaining KV and T-100 tanks attempted to guard the tank while recovery attempts were made, but this proved fruitless, even when T-28 tanks were used for towing. The SMK was not recovered until the spring after the fighting ended, and even then it had to be disassembled and removed in pieces.

Combat experience in Finland confirmed the earlier state trials, and on 19 December 1939 the Defence Committee accepted the KV for service as the Red Army's new heavy tank. An initial production batch of 50 tanks was ordered from the Kirovskiy plant for delivery in 1940 with a re-designed turret. The fighting against the Finnish bunkers prompted the commander of the 7th Army in Finland, Gen. K. Meretskov, to request crash production of a howitzer tank mounting a 152 mm or 203 mm weapon. Four programmes were undertaken, though only one was completed in time to serve in Finland. A 130 mm B-13 high-velocity naval gun was fitted into a fixed casemate mount on one of the T-100 prototypes, called the T-100U (U: Ulushchenniy = Improved). This was completed in the spring of 1940 after the Russo-Finnish war ended, and later served during the defence of Moscow in the winter of 1941 as the SU-130Y 'Igrek'. There was a similar attempt to mount either a 152 mm Br-2 or 203 mm B-4 howitzer into a modified KV hull called Obiekt 212, but this was never finished due to the outbreak of war with Germany. There was also some consideration given to developing a turreted 152 mm gun on the T-100 chassis, called the T-100Z, but the shortcomings of this tank led to the abandonment of this proposal.

INSIDE THE KV-1

The KV-1 Model 1941 had a five-man crew: commander/loader, gunner, and assistant driver/mechanic in the turret; and a driver, and radio-operator/hull

The standard production model of the KV-1 before the war was the KV-1 Model 1940, armed with the F-32 76.2 mm gun. Some production vehicles were fitted with four detachable external fuel cells for carrying additional diesel fuel as seen here.

machine gunner in the hull. The driver sat in the centre of the hull, slightly to the right. When driving outside the combat area a small hatch could be latched up so as to provide direct vision. When closed down for action the driver used a small slit in the visor, but the shoddy quality of the protective laminated glass block made it difficult to see through. In view of its weight and the absence of any power assistance, the KV was very difficult to steer. The tank used a dry multi-plate clutch with a sliding mesh gearbox; the transmission was undoubtedly the most troublesome mechanical component of the KV and the most frequent source of breakdowns. The KV-1 was powered by a V-2K engine offering 600 hp (442 kW). Fuel for the engine was provided in three large cells inside the fighting compartment: two on the right side and one on the left.

A KV-1 Model 1940 of the 6th Mechanised Corps knocked out at Zelva, 33 km west of Slonim in July 1941. The 6th Mechanised Corps in Byelorussia had more KVs than any other Red Army formation in 1941. This tank has suffered numerous hits which did not penetrate. There is a single large hit on the rear side, probably from an 88 mm AA gun, which almost certainly knocked out this tank. (US National Archives)

The KV heavy tanks were among the most alarming new weapons encountered by the Wehrmacht in 1941 and this photo amply demonstrates why. The side of the turret shows about 30 hits without a penetration. The fatal blow to was most likely an 88 mm hit on the hull side. This KV-1 Model 1940 of the 2nd Tank Division was knocked out during fighting with the 6th Panzer Division in June 1941. (Helmut Ritgen)

The basic arrangement

The radio-operator sat to the left of the driver, and operated the hull-mounted DT 7.62 mm MG. While radios were usually issued only to company and platoon commanders in medium and light tank companies, most KVs were radio-equipped from the beginning of the war. This was usually the older 71-TK-3 set which operated at pre-set frequencies by use of plug-in condensers – a temperamental device. When the vehicle was abandoned it was the responsibility of the radio-operator to remove the hull MG for defensive use. Often only the commander had a side arm, so the other crewmen took handgrenades or one of the other MGs.

As mentioned earlier, the turret was arranged in the traditional, crude, 1930s fashion, without a turret basket and with the commander doubling as the loader. German tankers frequently commented that Soviet tanks behaved clumsily, oblivious to local terrain features which could be exploited for better protection, and quite blind to many targets. Platoon-sized units showed little cohesion, and some stumbled about with little apparent regard for enemy tanks or the other tanks in their own unit. While some of these failings are attributable to poor training, much of the fault lies with the poor turret layout. This could not be remedied simply by having the third turret crewman, the assistant driver mechanic, take over the loading functions since the rear station where the third crewman sat had no all-around vision devices for the commander ; tactically he would have been virtually blind.

The commander was provided with a PTK periscope which was nearly identical to the PT-4-7 periscope used by the gunner but without the illuminated ballistic reticles for aiming. In addition there was a periscope on the side and a view slit above the right-side pistol port. As well as loading the main gun, the commander was responsible for feeding the co-axial 7.62 mm DT MG as required. His tasks were made ludicrously complex by the poor ammunition layout. There were ten ready rounds within easy reach, five of which were clipped on each wall of the rear turret bustle; but once these were exhausted it was necessary to rip up the floor to get at additional rounds. In fact the floor was made up of 44 stacked two-round containers, with a rubberised pad covering them, for a total of 98 rounds of 76.2 mm ammunition. In combat the floor rapidly became a jumble of opened containers, floor pads and spent shell casings. This clutter was the more bothersome as the assistant driver/mechanic was positioned close behind the commander/loader when the gun was in operation. Normally he sat on a pad suspended from the turret rack immediately behind the gun, but when the gun was in use the deflector and attached shell casing bin were folded up, filling this space. This seat was moved behind the commander; unsurprisingly, some KV tankers preferred only a four-man crew. In fact, by 1942, five-man crews for the KV became rare due to personnel shortages, and some KVs were operated by as few as three men, the radio-operator being the next position abandoned.

The principal functions of the assistant driver were

Probably the most famous encounter between the Wehrmacht and the new KV heavy tanks took place near Rasyeinyia when this single KV-2 Dreadnought stalled the 6th Panzer Division for several days by blocking a key crossroads. The thick armour of the KV-2 was impregnable to German tank fire, and only vulnerable to the superlative 88 mm AA gun. (US National Archives)

to relieve the driver when he became exhausted using the demanding clutch-and-brake steering system, and to take care of routine maintenance when halted. On the move he was usually assigned to the roof-mounted anti-aircraft DT MG located on the hatch ring, but the commander would often claim this position in order to get a better view. During combat he was assigned to the rear turret MG to keep infantry off the tank.

The Germans had a number of anti-tank mines which could disable a KV if properly positioned, and special care was needed when moving in towns or wooded areas where enemy infantry could approach the vehicle close-up unseen.

The gunner sat in the left-front corner of the turret opposite the commander. He was provided with two sighting instruments for the gun, a PT-4-7 periscopic sight with illuminated reticles, and a x2.5 power TMFD direct telescopic sight which was articulated with the gun's elevation. The telescopic sight was usually used when firing the main gun since it had better light transmission while the PT-4-7 was used for general target acquisition and observation since it could be traversed and had a wider field of view. The gunner elevated the gun with his right arm using a geared wheel, and could traverse the turret manually with his left arm or by using electric traverse. The electric traverse mechanism had three speeds, the fastest traversing 360° in 70 seconds, the slowest (for fine adjustments) in 120 seconds.

The engine

The KV-1 was powered by the same V-2 diesel engine as the T-34, providing 600 hp, but designated as the V-2K when adapted to the KV powertrain. Early verdons had a maximum road speed of 35 km/h (22 mph), but the up-armoured KV-1 Model 1941 was slower at 28 km/h (17 mph). The KV's torsion bar suspension gave a better ride than the Christie spring arrangement on the T-34. Wide tracks offered better floatation on soft soil or snow than the narrow tracks of contemporary German tanks. British and US evaluations of the KV found the design to be simple and robust. The finish was often poor, though not on moving parts where it was important. The quality of the armour was found to be excellent.

Armament

The ZIS-5 main gun used in the KV-1 was virtually identical to the F-34 used on the T-34, the designation merely acknowledging the mounting used in the KV. In fact, many parts of the ZIS-5 were labelled F-34. This was the longest of the three 76.2 mm guns fitted to the KV-1, the initial L-11 having a length of 30.5 calibres, the F-32 being 39 calibres, and the ZIS-5 being 41.5 calibres. The ammunition load on the KV progressively declined from 116 rounds on early machines to 111, and finally to 98 on the KV-1 Model 1941. The usual mixture was 24 rounds of AP and 74 rounds of HE-fragmentation, but of course in the field this varied enormously. At the beginning of the war, the standard AP round was the BR-350A which had an initial velocity of 662 m/sec, weighed 6.3 kg, and could penetrate 69 mm of armour at 500 m, more than adequate against the PzKpfw IV Ausf.F which had 50 mm frontal armour. By the spring of 1943, the Germans had boosted the armour of the PzKpfw IV to 80 mm, and the Russians followed suit with the high-velocity BR-350P AP projectile which had an initial velocity of 965 m/sec, weighed 3.02 kg, and could penetrate 92 mm of armour at 500 m. This improved round was lighter and more compact, which increased velocity, while its tungsten carbide core enhanced penetration. The standard HE round was the OF-350, a 6.2 kg projectile with a 0.7 kg TNT filler and contact fuze.

The KV-2 heavy tank

As mentioned earlier, the Finnish experience led to a requirement for a bunker-busting tank. The fourth of these projects was headed by N.L. Dukhov, and mounted a modified M-10 152 mm howitzer into a new, larger turret. A prototype was ready by the end of January 1940 and was subjected to impromptu trials near the Kirovskiy Plant. Although it had flaws, production of a small batch of four tanks was ordered to start immediately. At first this type was known as the 'large turret' KV (KV s bolshoi bashnei), but soon

In April 1941, the Red Army began a crash programme to up-armour the KV-1 based on faulty intelligence about German tank guns. This appliqué armour was distinctive due to the large bolt heads used to attach it to the side of the tank turret. This is the last surviving example of the KV-1 s ekranami, preserved at the Finnish armour museum at Parola. The Finnish army captured a single tank of this type in 1941 and put it back in service.

afterwards, it was redesignated as KV-2. It was popularly called the 'Dreadnought' by Soviet tankers. In mid-February, the first two vehicles were dispatched to the 20th Armoured Brigade in Finland. They were used in attacking Finnish bunkers, and one tank was

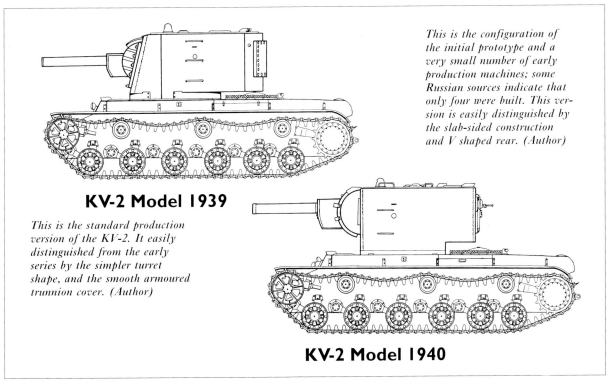

KV-2 Model 1939

This is the standard production version of the KV-2. It easily distinguished from the early series by the simpler turret shape, and the smooth armoured trunnion cover. (Author)

This is the configuration of the initial prototype and a very small number of early production machines; some Russian sources indicate that only four were built. This version is easily distinguished by the slab-sided construction and V shaped rear. (Author)

KV-2 Model 1940

The April 1941 'gun scare' led to the development of an up-armoured turret for the KV-1, which began to be manufac-tured in the summer of 1941. This is a tank straight from the Kirovskiy Plant in Leningrad, being sent to the nearby front to defend the city in the autumn of 1941 shortly before the plant was evacuated. The political slogan on the turret side reads 'We defend the Conquests of October', referring to the 1917 Bolshevik revolution in the city.

hit 48 times without a penetration. The KV-2 was accepted for series production in the latter half of 1940.

The KV-2 was intended as a heavy breakthrough tank, to help penetrate enemy defences reinforced with bunkers. The modified M-10 Model 1938/40 howitzer could fire a 52 kg (114 lb) projectile at 436 m/sec that was capable of penetrating 72 mm of steel armour at 1500 m. There was also a special 40 kg concrete pene-trating round for attacking pillboxes. The tank could carry 36 rounds of ammunition, mainly in the rear tur-ret bustle. The turret was re-designed before series production began in 1940. The new turret had curved side panels. In addition, the tank fire controls were upgraded, the T-5 telescopic sight being replaced by a TOD-9 sight and the PT-5 periscopic sight being

replaced by a PT-9; the commander was also given a PT-K periscopic sight. The later production types also had a hull MG position fitted in for added protection. Compared to the five man crew on the KV-1, the KV-2 had six: commander, gun commander, assistant, gun-ner, driver/mechanic and machine gunner/radioman. A total of 334 KV-2s were manufactured before produc-tion ceased in October 1941.

Improving the KV-1

The first KV-1 tanks were ready to be issued to the troops in the summer of 1940. Although the initial pro-duction order for the KV was for only 50 vehicles in 1940, its success in Finland led to this being increased. In total, 243 tanks were manufactured in 1940: 141 KV-1 and 102 KV-2. KV production also began at the Chelyabinsk Tractor Plant (ChTZ); the first test exam-ple from this plant was completed on 31 December 1940 and series production began slowly in the spring of 1941. The early production KVs were plagued by engine and transmission problems. The engine did not provide its rated horsepower and the vehicle was diffi-cult to steer. The KV-1 was scheduled to be fitted with the improved F-32 76.2 mm gun being designed by the P.F. Muravyev team at the Grabin central artillery design bureau at Artillery Plant Nr. 92 in Gorki, but due to delays, the short L-11 gun was used on the initial production run. The F-32 gun finally became available later in 1940, resulting in the KV-1 Model 1940.

In early 1941, the Grabin artillery bureau was also developing an improved, lengthened 76.2 mm gun for the new T-34 medium tank, called the F-34. The F-34 entered production in the spring of 1941, and began to be mounted on some T-34 tanks shortly afterwards. This led to the curious situation of the Red Army's medium tank having a slightly better gun than its counterpart heavy tank. As a result, after the German invasion approval was granted to up-arm the KV with a derivative of this gun, called the ZIS-5.

The up-armoured KV-3

German propaganda films from the 1940 campaign showed that the invaders had been able to penetrate the thick armour on the French Char B1 *bis* tank, and Soviet intelligence suggested that the Wehrmacht was adopting more powerful anti-tank guns. As a result, a requirement was approved for an up-armoured version of the KV series, the Obiekt 222, later known as the KV-3. The KV-3 had the hull and turret armour raised to 90 mm, increasing the overall weight of the tank from 47.5 tonnes to 51 tonnes. To compensate for the added weight, the improved 700 hp V-5 engine was used in place of the usual V-2K 600 hp diesel. It was planned to use the new ZIS-5 76.2 mm gun, and the commander was given a special observation cupola. A prototype was completed with the F-32 gun and subjected to trials in early 1941.

The KV-3 was offically accepted for service in May 1941, shortly before the outbreak of the war, still armed with the F-32 gun. It was planned to transition production at the Kirovskiy Plant from the KV-1 to the KV-3 in August 1941, but this never transpired due to the war. However, the KV-3 did show that the Red Army recognised some of the defects in the basic KV design (particularly its crew configuration), and had plans to remedy them before the war intervened. With the KV-3 abandoned, the decision was made to re-arm the KV-1 with the improved ZIS-5 gun, resulting in the KV-1 Model 1941.

The scare over purported new German tank guns in the spring of 1941 led to a crash programme to fit appliqué armour to the KV-1 Model 1940. Since the factories were not capable of handling any thicker armour it was decided to attach appliqué plates to the turret with large rivets. These were sometimes called KV-1 s ekranami (literally, KV with screens) and are referred to here as KV-1 (appliqué) Model 1941; they are sometimes called KV-1E. These 35 mm appliqué plates were riveted to the turret with narrow spacing so

The Obiekt 220 was an attempt to further modernise the KV series. The new turret was armed with an 85 mm gun, though a 107 mm gun was planned. The turret was lengthened, and a new more powerful engine installed. Roughly comparable to the later German Tiger I tank, the Obiekt 220 never entered production as the Soviet Union decided to concentrate on quantity rather than quality.

as to combat certain new armour-piercing (AP) rounds. The plates were most noticeable on the turret sides and front, though later batches had panels on the hull sides, both above and below the fender line, and had splash-strips added around the turret ring.

Super heavy tanks

There was also an interest to develop a version of the KV armed with a more effective gun, and even thicker

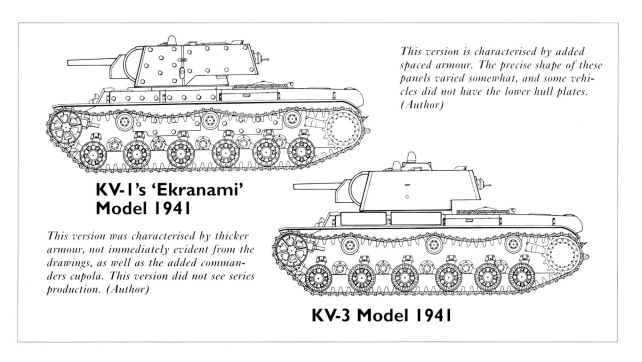

KV-1's 'Ekranami' Model 1941

This version was characterised by thicker armour, not immediately evident from the drawings, as well as the added commanders cupola. This version did not see series production. (Author)

This version is characterised by added spaced armour. The precise shape of these panels varied somewhat, and some vehicles did not have the lower hull plates. (Author)

KV-3 Model 1941

There was a plan to mount the new F-39 107 mm tank gun on the KV series. A series of firing trials were held near Moscow with Stalin attending, with the gun mounted on a KV-2 tank. But 'Barbarossa' demonstrated that Marshal Kulik's estimates about the thickness of German tank armour were wildly exaggerated, and the project was dropped.

armour. This programme was undertaken as Obiekt 220. The initial plan was to arm the Obiekt 220 with the new F-30 85 mm gun, derived from the 85 mm anti-aircraft (AA) gun. But in early 1941, a controversy erupted in the leadership of the Red Army that caused considerable turmoil in this and other tank gun programmes. Based on some sketchy intelligence information, Marshal I. Kulik, head of the Main Artillery Directorate (GAU), convinced himself that the Germans had re-armoured its tanks to 100 mm or more. Kulik insisted that new German tank armour would be thick enough to render the new ZIS-2 57 mm anti-tank gun and F-32 76.2 mm tank gun ineffective, and wanted to halt all production in favour the ZIS-6 107 mm anti-tank gun and F-39 107 mm tank gun. The heads of the tank and armament industry were opposed to this, arguing that Kulik's information was unreliable. Even if true, thicker armour could be countered by improved ammunition or an 85 mm gun compatible with existing ammunitions. Furthermore, the industry heads were concerned that such a decision would disrupt the manufacture of critical tank and anti-tank guns at the worst possible moment, with the threat of war looming on the horizon. In March 1941, after a series of high level meetings, Kulik's view finally prevailed. This turn of events had unfortunate repercussions, as the production of critical anti-tank guns and tank ammunition was halted while waiting for the new gun design to be completed. As a result, on 5 April 1941, plans to arm the Obiekt 220 with an 85 mm gun were dropped in favour of the F-39 107 mm gun and the Grabin artillery design team was ordered to accelerate development work.

The Obiekt 220 was based on a lengthened KV-1 hull, and was supposed to be powered by a version of

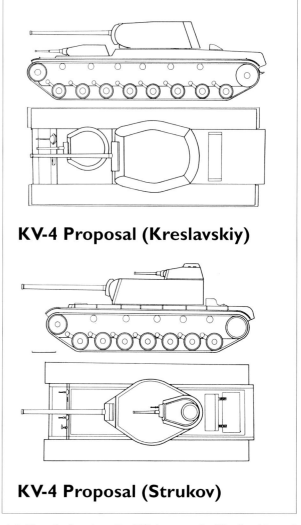

KV-4 Proposal (Kreslavskiy)

KV-4 Proposal (Strukov)

A 1:76 scale drawing of a KV-4 proposals (Kreslavskiy and Strukov). (Author)

the new M-40 aero engine, the V-2PUN, or an improved version of the V-2K engine, the V-2SN. One or more prototypes were completed in the early summer of 1941, but the F-39 tank gun was not completed until 15 July 1941. The new gun was mounted in a KV-2 for trials, but was never mounted in series production tanksdue to the outbreak of the war and the realization that German tank armour was not as thick as Kulik had erroneously claimed. As a result, the Obiekt 220 prototypes were armed with F-30 85 mm guns as originally planned. At least one later saw combat in the defence of Leningrad in 1941. The Obiekt 220 was never officially accepted for Red Army service, the general consensus being that it was too heavy and that it had powertrain problems. As a result, it was never given a 'KV' designation, although it was unofficially called the KV-220. It is worth noting, that in terms of armour and firepower it was similar in performance to the German Tiger I that appeared almost a year and a half later.

The KV-4 and -5 models

The controversy caused by Kulik's mistaken intelligence prompted further work on super-heavy tanks. There had been various schemes throughout the 1930s to develop 100 ton, or even larger, tanks. When Stalin decided to press ahead with a 107 mm tank gun, a

much larger tank would be needed to accommodate it. Two programmes were undertaken: the KV-4 (Obiekt 224) in the 92-tonne category and the KV-5 (obiekt 225) in the 150-tonne category. The KV-4 would be armed with the F-39 107 mm gun, have 130 mm frontal armour and 125mm side armour, and have a lengthened hull with seven roadwheels. The KV-5 was essentially similar in armament, but would have 170-180 mm frontal armour and 150 mm side armour, and eight road wheels per side. There were no fewer than 22 design configurations proposed for the KV-4 and KV-5. Several engineers at SKB-2 in Leningrad offered designs, including a conventional single-turret configuration from N.F. Shashmurin. One M.I. Kreslavskiy design had the engine mounted in the centre of the hull behind the driver, while another (shown here) had a configuration similar to the SMK. The Strukov design had the turret mounted in the usual position in the centre of the hull, but topped off the 107 mm gun turret with a small turret armed with an additional 45 mm anti-tank gun. Few details of the KV-5 designs are known. The evacuation of the Kirovskiy Plant ended any further work on these projects by 15 August 1941. There was considerable doubt by many industry officials about the practicality of such tanks, since they would exceed the usual 55-tonne limit of Soviet railways. Even the SMK and T-100 tanks

A KV-1 Model 1940 with the up-armoured turret moves to the front in the autumn of 1941. By this time, some of the lessons of the summer fighting were already being applied to the KV, notably the need to protect the turret race by adding appliqué armour panels.

There were numerous experimental versions of the KV-1. This is a special chemical warfare vehicle, sometimes called KV-12, which had a gas dispensing system added at the rear of the tank on either side. This consisted of the four storage tanks and two spray assemblies. These could dispense either chemical agents or smoke. There was no major requirement for such a vehicle, and the project was eventually abandoned. (R. Ismagilov)

had proved to be extremely difficult to transport. Furthermore, there was scant experience with compact engines able to provide the type of power needed to propel such large tanks.

Discrepancies in supply

Production of the KV series through June 1941 had totalled over 700 tanks, of which 508 had been delivered to Red Army tank units by the time the Germans struck on 22 June 1941. The Soviet armoured force was in the midst of a major reorganisation, which didn't exactly help. In 1940, Stalin had planned for the formation of 29 mechanised corps with 61 tank divisions – wildly optimistic, considering the state of the Soviet armoured park. The new 1940 mechanised corps consisted of two tank divisions and one motorised division, totalling some 1,031 tanks. Each tank division had a proposed strength of 63 KV heavy tanks, 210 T-34 mediums, 147 BT-7 cruiser tanks, 19 T-26 infantry tanks, eight T-26 flamethrower tanks, 53 BA-10 armoured cars and 19 BA-20 armoured scout cars. There was supposed to be a battalion of 31 KVs in each tank regiment. This organisational structure would have required over 3,800 KV tanks – not available until well into 1942 given Soviet production plans.

Due to the vast discrepency between the proposed organisation and the actual inventory of vehicles, few tank divisions approached their official strength. The distribution of KV tanks was very uneven. For example, in the 15th Mechanised Corps, the 10th Tank Division had a full organisation of 63 KVs, while the neighbouring 37th Tank Division had only a single KV. There were only six mechanised corps with at least a single battalion of KV tanks, and the best

equipped corps in terms of KV strength, the 6th Mechanised Corps, had 114 KVs. The mechanised corps with the greatest KV strength were: 3rd (52 KVs); 4th (99); 6th (114); 8th (71); 15th (64); and 22nd (31). One of these (3 MK) was in the Baltic Military District, another (6 MK) was in the Western Special Military District in Byelorussia, and the remainder were in the western Ukraine with the Kiev Special Military District.

The new tank divisions enthusiastically welcomed the new T-34s and KVs, but many units received them so late that there was no time for proper training. For example, of the 508 KV tanks in service on 22 June 1941, 41 had been delivered in the four weeks before the outbreak of the war. Few KVs had more than ten hours of use before the outbreak of the war. There was only a tenth of the 76.2 mm tank ammunition required, and no one had informed many of the units receiving the KV-2 that they were expected to use old 09-30 152 mm concrete-penetrating ammunition in lieu of non-existent AP rounds. Some KV-2 units, for example the 41st Tank Division (22nd Mech. Corps), had no ammunition at all for their tanks.

In spite of these daunting handicaps, most Soviet tank crews were cocky and confident due to their impressive new tanks. Indeed, the KV had no equal anywhere else in the world. Its closest counterparts were the French Char B1 *bis*, a very archaic design compared to the KV, and the British Matlida, which was poorly armed. The heaviest German tank, the PzKpfw IV Ausf.D, was not particularly well armoured, and its short 75 mm gun was incapable of penetrating the KVs armour. Indeed, no German anti-tank gun of the period, even the new 50 mm PAK 38, could penetrate the KV under normal combat conditions. As was the case with the Char B1 *bis* in the 1940 campaign, the only German weapon capable of knocking out heavy tanks was the 88 mm AA gun.

OPERATIONAL HISTORY

The Wehrmacht launched Operation 'Barbarossa' on 22 June 1941. The Red Army was unprepared for the attack, as Stalin adamantly refused to believe the growing intelligence data that suggested a German attack was imminent. As a result, many units were scattered or in the process of moving to their forward deployment areas when the Germans invaded.

Defensive action on the Dubissa River

The first major engagements between KVs and panzers took place in Lithuania the following day. Col.Gen. F. I. Kuznetsov's North-West Front had two partially equipped Mechanised Corps, the 3rd commanded by Maj.Gen. Kurkin (with 52 KV tanks) and the 12th commanded by Maj.Gen. Shestopalov (with no KV tanks). The 3rd Mechanised Corps was immediately divided up: the 2nd Tank Div. was sent along with the 12th Mechanised Corps towards the Dubissa River to stop the German advance along the main Tilsit-Shauliya highway, and the 5th Tank Div. rushed south to the border town of Alitus. Heavy fighting engulfed the 2nd Tank Div., commanded by Gen. E.N. Solyalyankin, which ran head-on into lead elements of the 4th Panzer Group along the main highway, including the PzKpfw 35(t)s of the 6th Panzer Div. An attack was immediately launched by about 80 BT light tanks supported by 20 KVs and a small number of T-34s. Gen. Reinhardt, who commanded the 41st Panzer Corps, recalled the encounter with the KVs:

'A hundred of our tanks, about a third of which were PzKpfw IVs, took their places for a counter-attack. Part of the force found itself directly facing the enemy, but most of the force was on the flanks. From three sides, they pummelled the steel monsters, but attempts to destroy them were futile. To the contrary, soon it was our tanks that were being knocked out. After a prolonged combat with the Russian giants, the German armoured units began to withdraw to avoid being annihilated. Echeloned in length as well as in depth, the giant tanks approached closer and closer. One of these began approaching a Panzer that was trapped in a marshy pond. Without hesitation, the black monster simply rolled over it. At that moment, a German 15 cm howitzer arrived. When its commander shouted that the enemy tanks were approaching, they opened sustained fire without causing the least damage. One approached the howitzer to within 100 metres. They fired again and the projectile struck with full force. The tank halted as though struck by a bolt of lightning. "We've done it" the artillerymen thought, quite relieved. "Yes, we have done it", said the gun captain. But their expressions suddenly changed when one yelled out, "It's moving again!" There was no doubt this was so as as the gleaming tracks soon

One of the few special purpose versions of the KV-1 was the KV-8 flamethrower tank. This version substituted a flamethrower for the main gun, though an auxiliary 45 mm gun – disguised with a false barrel to look like the standard 76 mm gun – was retained to defend the tank. This is a German intelligence photo of a KV-8 captured in 1942.

In 1942 there were some experiments to mount artillery rockets on tanks such as this KV-1K. Two armoured boxes were fitted on the fenders, each containing two rail launchers for RS-82 Katyusha rockets. Ultimately, this idea was dropped, probably due to the inaccuracy of the rockets. (R. Ismagilov)

approached the howitzer, crushed it like a toy into the soil, and continued on its way as though this was the most natural thing in the world.'

Not only were the 37 mm tank guns of the PzKpfw 35(t)s ineffective, but more frightening was the fact that 75 mm fire from the 'Stubs' (PzKpfw IVs with short 75 mm guns) also proved ineffective, the most powerful weapon on German tanks of the period. The 2nd Tank Div. claimed 40 panzers destroyed, and an equal number of guns, many of which were 37 mm guns simply run over and crushed like the 105 mm howitzer. Some of the Soviet tanks simply had no ammunition.

The 2nd Tank Div. withdrew from the battlefield around Skaudvilye by midday, to meet up with the 12th Mech. Corps north of Rasyeinyia. By this time the division was nearly out of fuel and ammunition,

and many of the older tanks were in bad mechanical condition due to the forced march. The division reached the fields above the Dubissa River, but were threatened by the advance of the 6th Panzer Div., which had already seized Rasyeinyia and had at least two bridgeheads over the Dubissa. The bridgeheads were attacked, and Gen. Solyalyankin sent a single KV-2 and some infantry past the German positions on the river to sever their road connections with the rest of 6th Panzer in Rasyeinyia.

There was one battalion of Pz35(t)s at the northern bridgehead near Lydaverai, and another battalion further down the river. On the afternoon of 23 June the Lydaverai battalion realised it had been cut off, and sent some of the anti-tank guns from PzJg.Abt. 41 and 105 mm howitzers from Art. Regt. 76 to cover their southern flank in case the Russians tried to attack them

The crew of a KV-1 Model 1941 loads ammunition into the turret. This is **Besposhadniy** ('Merciless') of the 12th Tank Regiment, which is also shown in the colour plates. After several months in combat, the crew added kill claims to the turret rear in the form of small geometric symbols; stars represented knocked out German tanks.

When production of the KV-1 was switched to the Tankograd complex in Chelyabinsk, a new cast turret was introduced alongside the up-armoured welded turret. Another change was the substitution of the ZIS-5 76.2 mm gun for the earlier F-32. This is an early example of the KV-1 Model 1941, seen near Klin in January 1942, shortly after the Red Army counter-attacks which pushed the Germans back from the gates of Moscow. (Aksonov)

from the rear. The next morning a relief column from Rasyeinyia tried to link up with the isolated German battalion, but its 12 trucks were quickly blown apart by the KV-2, which had positioned itself to cover the fork in the road leading to both bridgeheads. Further attempts were equally fruitless, and the situation at the river was getting rather precarious.

Attacks on the isolated battalions were intense, and the 37 mm gun of the PzKpfw 35(t) was a peashooter against the KVs. Only the 105 mm howitzers of the artillery had any effect on the leviathans. The situation became so critical that 6th Panzer was obliged to request 1st Panzer to the west to begin attacks against the Russian flank.

In the afternoon a battery of brand new PAK 38 50 mm anti-tank guns were carefully moved up towards the KV from the bridgehead. The lead gun was only 600 yards away when it began firing and was soon joined by the others. The KV-2 was not in the least disturbed by a direct hit, nor by the six other rounds that struck in quick succession. It destroyed the first gun with a direct hit, followed by several more rounds that damaged the other guns. In the meantime an 88 mm AA gun from Flak. Abt. 298 was carefully pulled out of its emplacement near Rasyeinyia and camouflaged with branches. The half-track towing it moved

*A group of KV-1 tanks of the 116th Tank Brigade on the Western Front in May 1942. The nearest tank is a KV-1 Model 1941 with cast turret, and is named **Shchorts** after the Bolshevik Civil War hero. The further vehicle is a KV-1 Model 1941 (up-armoured welded turret) and is named **Bagration** after the Russian prince who fought in the Napoleonic wars. (Chernov)*

A colourfully marked KV-1 Model 1941 moves forward past a smouldering German PzKpfw IV on the Southwestern Front in 1942. This is one of the original KV-1 Model 1941 configurations with the early pattern welded turret, early style resilient roadwheels, and the initial pattern turret ring appliqué. The slogan on the turret is **Za Rodinu** *– 'For the Homeland'.*

carefully behind the wrecked trucks for concealment and the crew hastily lowered the gun off its limbers. The activity had been spotted by the KV, and when the '88' was only 900 metres away the Russian gunner destroyed it and the tractor with two direct hits. Relief parties were kept away by MG fire. That night a squad from Pz.Pioniere Bn.57 crept up to the KV, placed a double charge of explosive against the hull, and detonated it – only to duck as the KV began spraying the area with MG fire. A straggler from the team approached the vehicle and found that the charge had only broken the track and ripped up the fender without any effect on the armour. He placed a second small charge on the barrel, but this had negligible results.

While these futile attempts to clear the road to the Dubissa River continued, the largest tank battle during the drive on Leningrad was taking place in the thick forests and swampy fields to the north. The 1st Panzer Div. had come to the rescue of 6th Panzer by striking the western flank of the 12th Mechanised Corps and 2nd Tank Division. During the attack Pz. Gren. Rgt. 113 of 1st Panzer was nearly overrun by KV-2s and attempts by Pz.Jg. Bn.37 to stop them proved fruitless when the 'Dreadnoughts' promptly trampled their 37 mm guns.

The 1st Panzer was equipped largely with PzKpfw IIIs and IVs, and had a greater measure of success against the KVs than the ineffective PzKpfw 35(t)s of 6th Panzer. They were unable to penetrate the frontal armour of the KV, but under unusual circumstances could sometimes disable them. A tanker from Pz. Regt. 1 wrote of the 24 June encounter on the Dubissa:

'The KV-1 and KV-2, which we first met here, were quite something. Our companies commenced firing at 800 metres but it was ineffective. We moved closer and closer... soon we faced each other at 50-100 metres. A fantastic exchange of fire took place without any German success... our armour-piercing rounds simply bounced off them. They drove right through us towards the infantry and rear services. We turned around and followed behind, where we succeeded in knocking some of them out with special-purpose rounds (Pzgr 40) at very close range: 30-60 metres!' The artillery of the 6th Panzer Div. had positioned itself on the heights overlooking the battlefield and made up for the poor showing of the 35(t) tanks against the KVs. The PzKpfw 35(t)s took a heavy toll of the lighter BTs and T-26s. Caught between the two Panzer Divisions, the remnants of the Russian force were pushed into the swamps where they were easy targets. By nightfall, nearly 180 burning Soviet tanks littered the battlefield.'

Among the Soviet casualties were 29 KV-1s and KV-2s, one of which had been hit 70 times without a single penetration. During this one encounter, most of the surviving KV heavy tanks in the Baltic region had been eliminated. Freed of the threat from the north, a platoon of PzKpfw 35(t)s was dispatched the next day from the bridgehead and worked its way to a small wood near the lone KV-2 at the crossroads. They kept up a steady stream of fire to distract the Russian crew while another 88 mm gun was carefully brought up from Rasyeinyia. When in position it opened fire, scoring six direct hits. The tank crews dismounted to inspect the KV, which had not even burned. On reaching the tank they were appalled to notice that only two

of the six 88 mm rounds had penetrated the armour. There were seven small gouges from the 50 mm strikes, but there was no damage evident from their 37 mm guns. As a couple of the tankers climbed on board, the gun began moving towards them. An engineer who had accompanied them had the presence of mind to drop a couple of grenades through the holes in the turret rear, finally putting an end to this troublesome roadblock. This single KV had played a prominent role in delaying the advance of Panzergruppe 4 on Leningrad by forcing the diversion of the 1st Panzer Div. from its rapid drive to help out 6th Panzer, and prevented the destruction of the immobile 2nd Tank Division, if only for a day.

The KV also played a prominent role in the enormous tank mêlée at Brody-Dubno in Ukraine. But as at Rasyeinyia, they could not decisively affect the outcome of these battles in view of the serious shortcomings of the Red Army at the time; they could only force the Panzer regiments, and especially the ill-protected infantry, to pay a heavy price for their advance. Gen.Maj. Morgunov, the armoured force commander in Ukraine in 1941, wrote in a once secret report: 'Special mention should be made of the good work of

During the war, Soviet tank repair facilities overhauled more than 400,000 armoured vehicles, many tanks being rebuilt several times during their career. This is a KV-1 Model 1941 (cast turret) being repaired at the Serp i Molot Plant in Moscow in 1942. This appears to be an example of one of the earliest configurations of cast-turreted KV-1 Model 1941, as it retains the initial resilient steel roadwheels. Most tanks of this type used the later spoked roadwheels.

the 4th, 8th and 15th Mechanised Corps who showed that a single KV tank was worth 10-14 enemy tanks in battle.' Army commanders, appreciating the near invulnerability of the KV, pleaded for more.

Maj.Gen. K. Rokossovskiy recalled in his memoirs: 'The KV tanks literally stunned the enemy. They withstood the fire of every type of gun that the German tanks were armed with.

But what a sight they were on returning from combat. Their armour was pock-marked all over and sometimes even their barrels were pierced.' Gen. I. Kh. Bagramyan recalled an incident during the fighting inside the town of Berdichev by the 10th Tank Div. when a single KV-1 commanded by Lt. I.N. Zhalin knocked out eight German tanks, even though it had

The crew of a KV-1 Model 1941 (cast turret) tank named **Istrebitel** ('Fighter') on the Kalinin Front in northern Russia in the winter of 1942. The tank commander, Jr. Lt. I.M. Tovstikh, is in the foreground. The tank is carrying a large piece of timber, which was used as an unditching beam to extract the tank from soft ground. (P.I. Maksimov)

suffered over three dozen direct hits at extremely close range. In late July Lt.Gen. A. Yeremenko sent a report back to Col.Gen. D.G. Pavlov, commander of the Western Front: 'Handled by brave men, the KV tanks can do wonders. In the sector of the 107th Motorised Infantry Division we sent a KV to silence an enemy anti-tank battery.

It squashed the artillery, rolled up and down the enemy's gun emplacements, was hit more than 200 times, but the armour was unpierced even though it had been the target of guns of all types. Often our tanks went out of action due to the hesitant and unsure conduct of their crews rather than direct hits.

For this reason we subsequently manned the KV tanks with hand-picked crews.' Battle losses of KVs were caused most often by German 105 mm howitzers or 88 mm guns. Although the 105 mm howitzer could not penetrate the armour of the KV, it could blow off its tracks. The new 50 mm PAK 38 could penetrate the 75 mm side armour of the KV at close ranges, but only with the special Pzgr 40 projectile.

Lack of trained crews

In spite of the exceptional performance of the KV tanks on many individual occasions, the overall impact of the KV tanks on the 1941 fighting was negligible. Their technical superiority could not overcome the overwhelming tactical and operational shortcomings of the Red Army in the summer of 1941. Commanders singled out several reasons for the problems with the KV. The most serious was the general lack of training for the crews. A report from Ukraine on 8 July noted:

'There were exceptionally great losses of KV-2 tanks in the 41st Tank Division. Of the 31 tanks available to the division, by 6 July 1941 only nine remain. The enemy knocked out five, 12 were blown up by their own crews, and five were sent for major repairs. The heavy losses of the KV tanks are attributable primarily to the poor technical training of the crews, by their poor knowledge of the tank systems, as well as a by an absence of spare parts. When the crews were unable to eliminate malfunctions on stalled KV tanks, there were many occasions when they had to blow them up.'

The relative novelty of the tank meant that few crews could carry out anything more than minor maintenance. After being subjected to long road marches, particularly in the Ukraine, the tanks soon required significant maintenance at a time when their were neither the skilled crews nor spare parts to carry them out. For example, the commander of the relatively well equipped 8th Mechanised Corps, Gen.Lt. D.I. Ryabyshev reported: 'From 22-26 June 1941, we carried out movements much beyond normal forced marches without being able to observe the elementary prescribed requirements for maintaining equipment and resting personnel.

The equipment arrived at the battlefield after having covered distances of 500 km. As a result of this, 40 to 50 per cent of the tanks were broken down for technical reasons... and abandoned on the routes of march of the division. As the consequence of such rapid marches, the remaining tanks were technically unprepared for combat.' The 37th Tank Division covered 1500 km in less than two weeks, suffering serious

mechanical breakdowns. At the time, the average service life for new Soviet tanks was about 1000-1500 km before factory rebuilding was necessary.

The 10th Tank Division (15th Mech. Corps) had to endure fruitless forced marches trying to catch the rapidly moving panzer columns. The 10th Tank Division lost 56 of its 63 KVs in fighting through early August, of which 11 were knocked out in combat, 11 went missing in action, and 34 were abandoned or scuttled due to breakdowns.

It appears that this pattern occured in most other units judging from surviving records. For example, the 8th Tank Division lost 43 of their 50 KVs: 13 in com-

This detail view of a preserved museum vehicle in Russia shows four of the different styles of road-wheels used on the KV heavy tank. The roadwheel at the right is the initial pattern used in 1939-41 which contained a resilient rubber ring inside for cushioning. The spoked wheel at the extreme left began to replace it in the autumn of 1941 and became the standard type on KV-1 Model 1941 and Model 1942 tanks. The wheel second from the right is one of the initial types used on the KV-1S, and the wheel third from the right is another KV-1S variation. (Janusz Magnuski)

bat, two which became stuck in swamps and 28 which were abandoned or destroyed by their crews due to mechanical breakdowns.

In 1942, an up-armoured cast turret was introduced with increased armour thickness. This is most easily distinguished by the added armour collar around the rear turret MG. The hull armour was also thickened, leading to a change in the rear shape, with a simple angled rear rather than the rounded rear used earlier. This KV-1 Model 1942 is currently preserved at the Parola tank museum in Finland.

In 1942, the Kotin design bureau began work on the KV-13 'universal tank', an attempt to combine the heavier armour of the KV with the smaller size and lighter weight of the T-34. This is the KV-13T version, which used T-34 track. The KV-13 and the competitive T-43 universal tank were a dead end, as the introduction of the Tiger and Panther made it clear that a new gun, not thicker armour, was needed. (Slava Shpakovskiy)

Mechanical and design weaknesses

The KVs suffered a significantly higher rate of loss due to mechanical problems than other new tanks such as the T-34, according to available records. One of the main problems was the clutch and powertrains. A 1941 field report complained that 'the impact of projectiles jams the turret race and the armoured vision ports; the diesel engine has little reserve power leading to the motor becoming overworked, and the master clutch and steering often breakdown.'

A German training course at Wunsdorf in early 1942 summarised the Wehrmacht assessment of captured KVs which largely concurred with the view of Russian commanders: 'Mechanically, this tank is a poor job. Gears can only be shifted and engaged at the halt, so the maximum speed of 35 km/h is an illusion. The clutch is too lightly constructed. Almost all abandoned tanks had clutch problems.'

The combat utility of the KV was also undermined by several other factors, especially poor crew layout and poor vision devices. The turret was manned by three men as on German tanks, but their functions were different. The commander sat on the right side of the gun and doubled as the loader. The third turret crewman was intended to man the rear turret MG.

The vehicle hatch was located over the machine gunner, not the commander, so that the tank commander was not able to ride with his head outside the tank, surveying the terrain as was the German practice. Furthermore, Soviet vision devices were poor; the armoured glass in the driver's visor was sub-standard, being full of air bubbles.

*In the autumn of 1942, the 5th Guards Heavy Tank Regiment was given 21 new KV-1S tanks, purchased with donations from the Glavsevmorput (GUSMP), the organisation responsible for Arctic sea voyages. These tanks were marked with the inscription **Sovyetskikh Polyarnik** – 'Soviet Arctic Explorer'. The regiment was committed at Stalingrad in December 1942 near Kazachiy Kurgan, north-west of the city, in support of the 65th Army of the Don Front.*

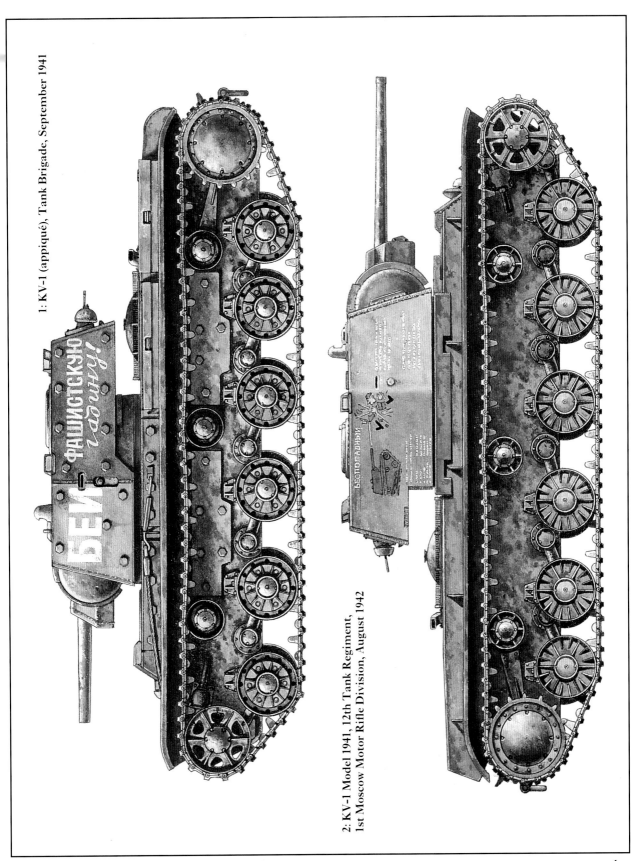

1: KV-1 (appliqué), Tank Brigade, September 1941

2: KV-1 Model 1941, 12th Tank Regiment,
1st Moscow Motor Rifle Division, August 1942

A

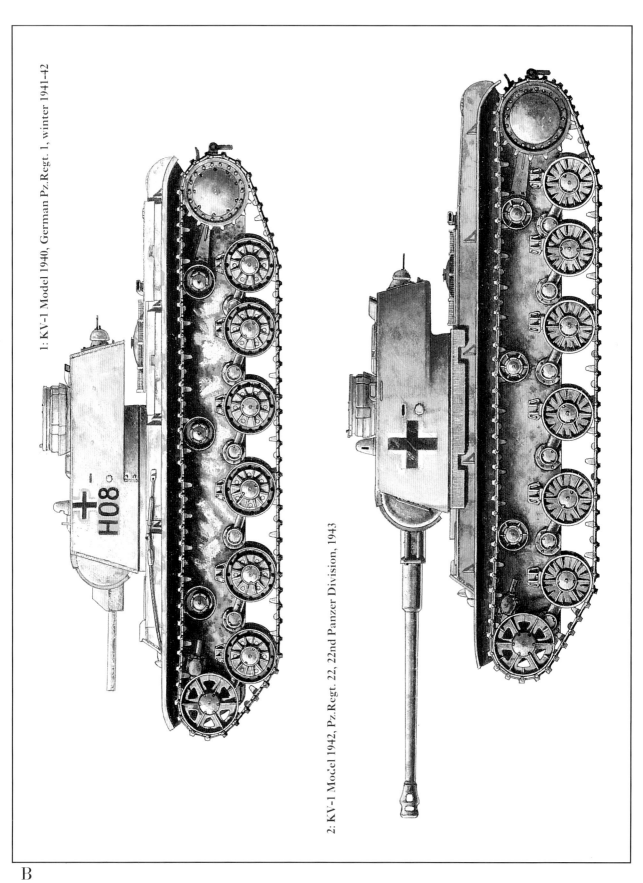

1: KV-1 Model 1940, German Pz.Regt. 1, winter 1941–42

2: KV-1 Model 1942, Pz.Regt. 22, 22nd Panzer Division, 1943

B

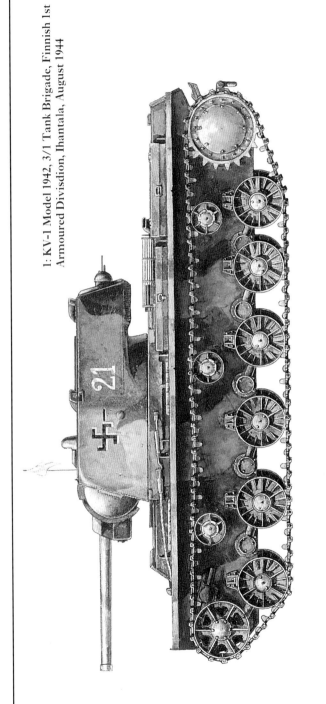

1: KV-1 Model 1942, 3/1 Tank Brigade, Finnish 1st Armoured Divisdion, Ihantala, August 1944

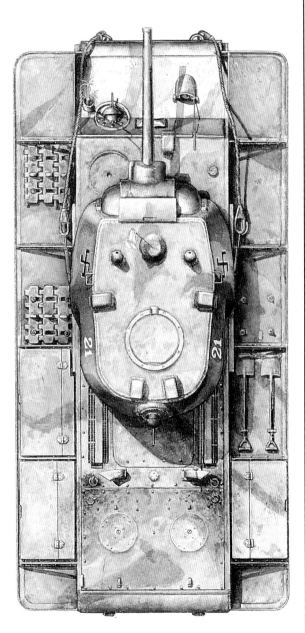

KV-1 MODEL 1941
Soviet Heavy Tank Regiment, 1942

SPECIFICATIONS

Crew: 5 (commander, gunner, auxiliary driver, driver/mechanic, radio-operator)
Combat weight: 47 tons
Power-to-weight ratio: 13 hp/T
Hull length: 22 ft. 2 in
Overall length: 22 ft 8 in
Width: 10 ft 11 in
Height: 9 ft 7 in
Engine: V-2K 4-stroke, V-type, 500 HP @180 rpm, 38.8 litre diesel engine
Transmission: Dry multi-plate main clutch, sliding mesh gearbox, multi-plate clutch braking turning mechanism , 5 gears forward, 1 reverse
Fuel capacity: 600 litres (158 gallons) internal
Max. speed (road): 21 mph
Max. speed (cross-country): 10 mph
Max. range: 155 miles
Fuel consumption: 2.4 L/km; 1 gal/mi
Fording depth: 5.2 ft
Armament: 76.2mm ZIS-5 rifled tank gun, 42 calibers long; three 7.62mm DT machine guns
Main gun ammunition: BR-350A armour piercing; OF-350 HE/frag; Sh-350A shrapnel
Muzzle velocity: 2,150 ft/sec (BR-350A)
Max. effective range: 1.5 miles
Stowed main gun rounds: 135 rounds
Gun depression/elevation: -4 to + 24 degrees
Armour: 75mm (hull basis); 75mm+26mm (hull nose); 75mm + 31mm (glacis); 40mm (belly); 32mm (hull rear); 95-100mm cast (turret front and sides); 30mm (turret roof)

KEY

1. 10-R Radio transceiver
2. Radio antenna with aerial spreader
3. Driver's accelerator pedal
4. Driver's left steering lever
5. Driver's protected glass view slit
6. Compressed air tanks for cold weather engine starting
7. Driver's clutch
8. Armoured gun mantlet
9. Gunner's turret traverse gear
10. Turret roof vent fan cover
11. PT-4-7 gunner's periscopic sight
12. Gun elevation wheel
13. Turret roof hatch
14. Breech of ZIS-5 76mm gun
15. Shell casing catcher/protective cage
16. DT 7.62mm anti-aircraft machine gun
17. Turret 76mm ammunition ready stowage
18. Armoured cover for turret vision periscopes
19. 7.62mm machine gun ammunition stowage
20. Rear 7.62mm DT machine gun
21. Machine gun mantlet
22. Gunner's seat
23. Turret race protective armour strip
24. Engine air filter
25. Engine access hatch
26. Right exhaust port
27. V-2K diesel engine
28. Engine radiator
29. Radiator air vent cover
30. Transmission access hatch
31. Transmission brake assembly
32. Dry multi-plate transmission
33. Drive sprocket
34. ZIP tool stowage box
35. Floor ammunition stowage boxes
36. Turret electrical conduit pipe
37. Turret floor protective mat
38. Gunner's firing pedal
39. Suspension arm shock absorber
40. Left side 135 litre fuel tank
41. Front hull 7.62mm machine gun ammunition stowage
42. Mechanical linkage between driver's clutch and transmission
43. Driver's seat
44. Main road wheel
45. Idler wheel
46. Manganese-chromium steel track link

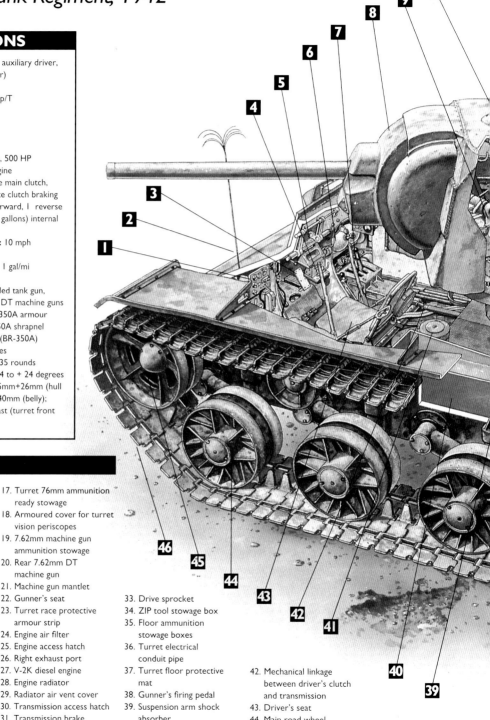

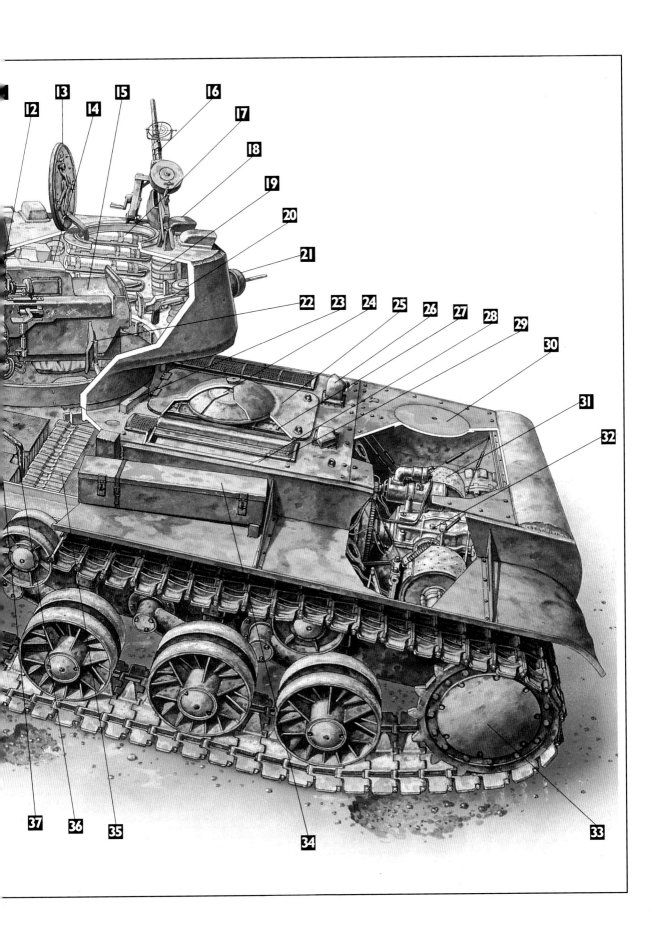

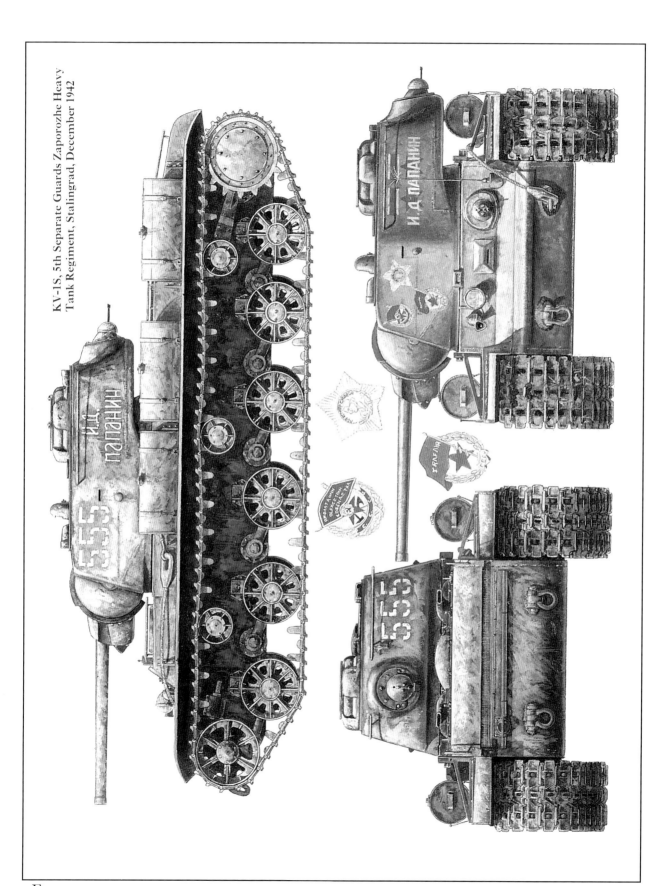

KV-1S, 5th Separate Guards Zaporozhe Heavy
Tank Regiment, Stalingrad, December 1942

E

1: KV-8S Model 1943, Flamethrower Tank Regiment, summer 1944

KV-1S, Heavy Tank Regiment, Battle of Berlin, April 1945

This detail view shows the rear of the heavily revised turret of the KV-1S, with a vision cupola for the commander on the left side, and a new separate hatch for the loader on the right. This turret was considerably smaller than the cast turret previously used on the KV-1 Model 1942.

The German assessment was that: 'Facilities for observation are worse than in our tanks. The driver's vision is incredibly bad.' The designers had recognised this problem as was evident in the KV-3 and Obiekt 220 design, but it was realised too late to have any effect on the 1941 fighting. This lack of appreciation for the tactical impact of poor turret configuration was shared with most Red Army tanks (see New Vanguard 9: *The T-34-76 Medium Tank*). As a result, Red Army tanks had difficulty locating and identifying the enemy. In tank combat, the KV commander was overwhelmed with duties, being forced to share his time between handling his vehicle with other tanks in the platoon as well as loading the gun. As a result, Red Army tank attacks tended to be more poorly co-ordinated than German actions.

By late summer, the Red Army's armoured force had suffered staggering losses, and there were few KVs still left in service. On 15 July, STAVKA (Soviet High Command), was obliged to recognise the obvious and disband the mechanised corps. Of the 22,000 tanks in existence at the beginning of 'Barbarossa', it is unlikely that more than 1,500 remained operational. In place of the huge and unwieldy mechanised corps, STAVKA created tank brigades as the largest tactical armoured formation.

These new brigades were organised around a tank regiment and a motor rifle battalion with a nominal strength of 93 tanks. The tank regiment included a company of seven KV tanks, a company of 22 T-34 tanks, and the remainder of the unit was filled out with whatever light tanks were available.

The Urals Evacuation

As the tanks of Panzergruppe 4 raced up the Baltic coast towards Leningrad in July, the main KV production plant was threatened with capture. Efforts began to evacuate the entire facility east to Chelyabinsk where a second production line had been open since earlier in the year. Nevertheless, the heavy losses from the summer campaign forced the Russians to hold out as long as possible before moving the plant. In August 1941, the Kharkov engine factory that provided V-2 diesels to the Leningrad plant had to be abandoned, causing a powerplant shortage. As a result, in 1941 about 100 KVs were built with M-17 petrol engines, the type used previously in the T-35 heavy tank.

On 10 September 1941, the Kirovskiy plant in Leningrad was hit by a major Luftwaffe air raid, further impeding production. The evacuation of the Kirovskiy Plant to Chelyabinsk was completed in mid October 1941. The equipment and workers from this plant were merged with parts of the Kharkov Diesel Works and the Chelyabinsk Tractor Factory (ChTZ) to form a new complex Chelyabiusk Heavy Machinery Factory No.100 (Ch ZTM), popularly called Tankograd (Tank City).

The successful relocation of the Kirovskiy Plant and others like it was an accomplishment as important as the victory at the gates of Moscow that winter. The new factories were free from the ravages of German bombers, and began to provide a stream of new tanks to rebuild the Red Army's shattered armoured formations. In 1941, 1,358 KVs were manufactured, of which 1,121 were KV-1s, 232 KV-2s, and the remainder prototypes.

Periodic rebuilding of KV tanks at special repair factories sometimes led to a mixture of subcomponents not originally intended by the designers. This KV-1 in action with the 2nd Baltic Front in Latvia in 1944 consists of a KV-1S hull, but with an old up-armoured welded turret from a KV-1 Model 1941. This hybrid was probably created after the original KV-1S turret was penetrated by German shell fire, and proved unrepairable.

KV-1 (up-armoured welded turret) Model 1941

Right: *A 1:76 scale drawing of a KV-1 Model 1941 (up-armoured welded turret). The KV-1 Model 1941 was characterised by the new ZIS-5 76mm gun. The initial production vehicle used the same turret as the KV-1 Model 1940. However, the most common production version in 1941 as shown here used the up-armoured welded turret, characterised by the lower rear sides of the turret which did not wrap around the ring. (Author)*

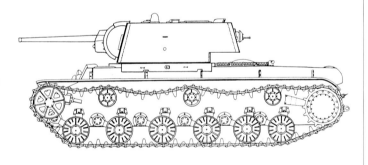

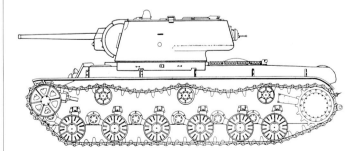

KV-1 (cast turret) Model 1941

Left: *A 1:76 scale drawing of a KV-1 Model 1941 (cast turret). The KV-1 Model 1941 was also manufactured with a cast turret as shown here. By this time, the configuration of the turret splash strips had become fairly standard. (Author)*

IMPROVEMENTS IN ARMAMENT

The KV-1S remained in service until the end of the Second World War. This KV-1S is supporting an infantry attack on the Karelian isthmus in June 1944, when the Red Army finally forced Finland out of the war. (Suchatov)

The principal aim of Kotin's SKB-2 design team became the simplification of the KV to maximise production. Improvements were introduced only if they did not interfere with manufacture. Before the factory evacuation, efforts were underway to up-armour the turret in response to the April 1941 armour scare promoted by Marshal Kulik. The original production turret had 90 mm frontal armour and 75 mm side plates. The new turret, based on that developed for the KV-3, was 90-120 mm in the front, and 95 mm on the sides. The up-armoured turret looked similar to the first welded production type apart from the shape under the turret overhang, where the panel continued further to the rear rather than bending around the turret race. Based on reports from the front already cited, small strips of appliqué armour were welded around the turret to prevent it from jamming when hit. At the end of 1941, a new, simpler, spoked roadwheel was introduced which used less rubber than the original type.

In July 1941, the first KV-1 Model 1941s were manufactured, armed with the new ZIS-5 76.2 mm gun. These were produced alongside KV-1 Model 1940s until supplies of the original F-32 gun were exhausted. A small number of these were produced with the original welded turret, but most were produced with the up-armoured turret. It is difficult to categorise these many variations as the Red Army did not codify them with elaborate designations like those employed by the Wehrmacht's Waffenamt. They made scanty use of the rough model/year designation system, and with little regularity. The external appearance of KVs after the evacuation became more erratic due to the variety of supplies of subcomponents. Both Chelyabinsk and the Uralmash Plant in Sverdlovsk produced KV hulls, and there were also at least two turret subcontractors, one producing cast and the other welded turrets. Supplies of older F-32 gun continued to trickle into Chelyabinsk, so it was possible to see a KV-1 with early hull and turret production features but with the new ZIS-5 gun, alongside a KV-1 with the new hull and turret features, but armed with the outdated F-32 gun. Shortages of radios led to some tanks being fitted with aircraft radios.

By 1942, all KV-1s were manufactured with the ZIS-5 gun, although some received the similar F-34 76.2 mm gun from the T-34 due to factory shortages of the other weapon. There were many small detail changes on the KV as hull details were improved. As was the case with the T-34, a cast turret was developed for the KV to speed production. This was equivalent to the uparmoured welded turret, and had sides 100 mm thick. Later in 1942, the KV was further up-armoured to counter improvements in German tank and anti-tank guns, notably the long 75 mm gun on the PzKpfw IV and the new PAK 40 75 mm anti-tank gun. The hull armour side plates were increased in thickness from 75 mm to 90 mm. The cast turret was improved by thickening it even further to 120 mm at the sides. This improved cast turret could be distinguished by a ring of armour around the rear turret MG, and subtleties of the casting at the front of the turret. This version is sometimes called the KV-1 Model 1942, though the Red Army never took great pains to designate subvariants.

Through 1942, efforts were made to simplify KV production in order to increase the number manufactured. This was fairly successful; the 1941 price for the tank of 635,000 roubles dropped to 295,000 roubles in 1942 and 225,000 roubles in 1943. But the emphasis on sheer numbers inhibited some improvements, and sometimes led to shoddy workmanship. The awkward turret layout remained unchanged. The enormous pressure to keep up production often led to inadvertent mistakes. During 1943, there were frequent reports from the front of breakdowns caused by transmission gear teeth failure. It was finally discovered that the inexperienced factory workers (mostly young boys and, at best, semi-skilled men and women), were accidently using large discs of ShKh-15 chromium steel intended for bearing rings instead of the special KhN-4 chrome-

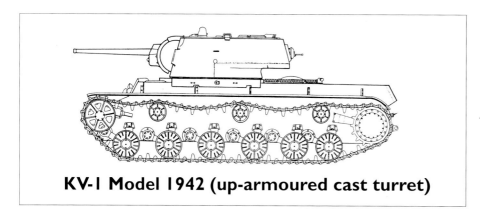

KV-1 Model 1942 (up-armoured cast turret)

This model was charac-terised by an improved cast turret with thicker armour. The shape of this turret is better appreciated by exam-ining photographs. However, the clearest distinguishing feature is a ring of armour around the rear turret machine gun. This vehicle uses the uparmoured hull, identifiable by the simple angled shape of the upper hull rear. (Author)

nickel-molybendium steel alloy intended for gear wheels. Both rough discs were similar in appearance before machining, and were located near one another on the factory floor.

The Red tank force revived

In late 1941/ early 1942, the KV-1s still had an enor-mous technological advantage over their German coun-terparts due to their thicker armour and superior gun. Although the Wehrmacht still dominated the battlefield through superior tactics and training, the KVs were often able to secure local successes.

On 19 August 1941, a platoon of four KV-1s of the 1st Tank Division successfully ambushed a German tank column advancing near the Voiskovitsy collective farm near Leningrad. The platoon leader, Sr.Lt. Zinoviy Kolobanov, knocked out the two lead tanks in the column. The following tanks apparently did not realise what had happened and continued to unwarily move forward.

Kolobanov's platoon moved into the midst of the German battalion, and in the melée that followed, Kolobanov destroyed a total of 22 German tanks, ram-ming at least one in the process. Kolobanov's tank was hit 135 times during the firefight. The other three KVs destroyed a total of 16 other German tanks. Kolobanov's feat made him the second highest ranking Soviet tank ace of the war.

Some of the most savage tank fighting took place in the approaches to Moscow starting in October 1941 as the Red Army attempted to prevent the German seizure of the capital. During the fighting, a KV-1 of the 89th Separate Tank Battalion commanded by Lt. Pavel Gudz knocked out ten tanks in fighting near Volokolamski, taking 29 hits from German tanks and anti-tank guns in the process. But the KV's real suc-cess came in encounters with German infantry. Most German infantry units were still equipped with the

PAK 36 37 mm anti-tank gun, which was nearly use-less against the T-34 and KV tanks. Even units defended by the new PAK 38 50 mm anti-tank gun struggled to stop a KV. Fortunately for the Wehrmacht, KVs were still few and far between in 1941 and early 1942, though they were greatly feared by German infantry.

Following the bloody débâcle of summer 1941 and the dogged resistance before Moscow and Leningrad in the winter of 1941-42, efforts began to rejuvenate the Soviet tank force. The August 1941 tank brigade estab-lishment was 93 tanks: 22 T-34s, seven KV-1s and 64 light tanks. In view of the huge losses suffered in 1941 these were optimistic figures and few brigades reached this strength. About 900 KVs were lost in fighting in 1941, leaving only about 600 on strength by the end of the year.

In September 1941, the tank brigade organisation was reduced to 67 tanks including seven KV-1s. Furthermore, the separate tank battalions formed to support infantry and cavalry units had KVs dropped from their establishment due to their scarcity. This led to an outcry from infantry commanders who prized KVs for their near invulnerability and psychological effect on the poorly armed German infantry.

The transfer of factories to the Urals caused a tem-porary drought in tanks, so that by February 1942, the tank brigade strength reached its nadir at a mere 27 tanks, of which ten were supposed to be KVs. This soon improved once the factories began increasing pro-duction; the nominal brigade strength in the spring was 46 tanks with ten KVs.

At this time the tank brigades were divided into two battalions, each with a light, a medium and a heavy company; the latter consisted of two platoons of two KVs each and a company commander's KV. Heavy KV companies usually led counter-attacks due to their excellent armour.

On average, factories and mobile repair bases rebuilt or overhauled every tank about four times. As war rages around the city, this KV-1S is receiving a new transmission gearbox at the Stalingrad Tractor Plant during in the autumn of 1942. (Sofin)

VARIANTS

During the winter of 1941-42, the relocated SKB-2 design bureau in Chelyabinsk began a series of design studies to improve the armament of the KV tank. An experimental assault gun mounting a Br-2 naval gun had been tested on a shortened KV chassis earlier in 1941, but this proved unsuccessful; no photo of this version appears to have survived.

KV-7 assault-gun

During 1941, Red Army units had encountered the German StuG III assault gun in considerable numbers, and a SKB-2 design team, headed by G.N. Moskvin, decided to go the Germans one better. The KV-7 was a scheme to arm an assault gun version of the KV with multiple guns instead of a single gun as on the StuG III. Two different versions were envisioned. The first type (sometimes called KV-6) was armed with a single 76 mm gun in the centre flanked by two 45 mm guns, with 93 rounds of 76 mm ammunition and 200 rounds of 45 mm ammunition. The guns could fire in salvo or separately, and the mounting permitted the triple armament to traverse 7° to either side. The second version was armed with two 76 mm guns mounted side by side, with a total of 300 rounds of 76 mm ammunition. The design of these types began on 14 November 1941 and were completed by the end of the month. They were hurriedly shipped to Moscow on 29 December 1941 for a demonstration to Stalin, being hastily

painted en route. Serious consideration was given to series produce one of the types, but there were lingering problems with the design, such as assymetrical forces on the trunnions when the guns were fired singly that damaged the mounting and knocked it out of boresight. Many of the designers at SKB-2 were skeptical of the concept, and one later wrote: 'The KV-7 was "technical adventurism": completely useless expenditure of energy and peoples' time, a waste of valuable resources, and a waste of a good deal of high-alloy steel.' Nor was Stalin very impressed with the idea. He scolded the designers and said: 'Why three guns? We only need one, but a better one!' As a result, the KV-7 idea was dropped.

KV-8 flamethrower

The KV-8 development work took place in Chelyabinsk in November 1941 alongside the KV-7 project. Flamethrower tanks were a standard feature of Soviet tank doctrine since the pre-war years, and they were used extensively in Finland. But they were based on T-26 light tanks which made them terribly vulnerable to enemy fire. Flamethrower mountings were planned for both the KV and T-34 tank. The Chelyabinsk designers decided to mount the ATO-41 flamethrower in the turret of the KV, while the T-34 designers mounted it in the hull in place of the MG. Experience in Finland had shown that tanks which were obviously flamethrowers tended to attract unfavourable attention from enemy anti-tank guns. Furthermore, when their fuel supply was exhausted they were practically defenceless. However, the space taken by the flamethrower precluded the use of the normal 76 mm gun. Instead, a compromise was accepted, with the flamethrower being mounted in a small armoured sleeve on the right side the gun mantlet, and a 45 mm Model 32/38 gun mounted in place of the 76 mm gun. Ingeniously, the 45 mm gun tube was disguised with a thicker false barrel to mimic the 76 mm weapon. The KV-8 carried 92 rounds of 45 mm ammunition, and 960 litres of fuel for the flamethrower. The flamethrower could fire three bursts every ten seconds, and each burst consumed 10 litres of fuel. The range of the flamethrower depended on the fuel: normal kerosene had a range of 60-65 m while a special mixture of kerosene and oil had a range of 90-100 m. The KV-8 was demonstrated to Stalin at the same time as the KV-8 and met with his enthusiastic approval. Production of the KV-8 flamethrower tank began in 1942. The main advantage of the KV flamethrower tank over the T-34 type was its greater fuel capacity, almost five times as much. Both types were used together in separate flamethrower tank battalions (sometimes called chemical tank battalions)

which had ten KV-8s in two companies, and 11 OT-34 tanks in one company. Although the flamethrower battalions were usually used in an offensive role to overcome bunkers in support of infantry units, their psychological value led to them being used in a wide range of other missions.

KV-9 howitzer

This was a KV-1 tank armed with the U-11, a special tank version of the M-30 122 mm howitzer. This tank was intended as an alternative to specialised self-propelled (SP) guns like the KV-7. The U-11 122 mm howitzer was viewed as a 'universal gun', capable of being used both for tank fighting and direct fire support. But this idea was not accepted by the tank troops,

The KV-1S named after I.D. Papanin served with the 5th Separate Guards Zaporozhe Heavy Tank Regiment. This photo was taken in the summer of 1943 in the Orel region during the armoured clashes around Kursk-Orel. Second from the left is the crew commander Lt. S. Nikolayev, while in the centre is the company commander, Sr.Lt. V. Panfeli. Illustrations of the markings of this tank at other times in its career are shown in The Plates. (Biryukov)

who were uneasy with the idea of a howitzer being used in tank fighting due to the arched trajectory of the projectile compared to the relatively flat trajectory of normal tank guns, which made aiming more difficult. The rate of fire was reduced due to the heavy weight of the projectile compared to the 76 mm round. In addition, only 48 rounds of ammunition could be carried, about half that of a normal KV-1. As a result, the project did not progress beyond prototypes. In 1943, the KV-9 turret later was mated to a KV-13 hull as a test-bed for the later IS Stalin heavy tank series.

KV-1K rocket launcher

Another effort to increase the firepower of the KV was the KV-1K. This was a standard tank fitted with launchers on both fenders for Katyusha rockets. There were two armoured boxes per side and launch rails for two RS-82 rockets per box. These were intended to provide supplementary firepower when attacking heavily reinforced positions. But the rockets were rather inaccurate, and the idea was dropped. Nothing is known of the KV-10 or KV-11 projects. There was also a project to mount a smoke and chemical agent dispenser on the KV tank, sometimes called the KV-12, but it did not enter series production.

TACTICAL PROBLEMS

By mid 1942 Soviet tank brigade commanders were having difficulties using their assortment of tanks in a cohesive fashion. Soviet tank brigades had at least three types of tanks: light tanks, T-34 medium tanks and KV heavy tanks. This was a logistical headache, and often presented tactical problems as well. The continued up-

In 1943 Nikolai Dukhov's team at Chelyabinsk attempted to up-arm the KV-1S with the Grabin S-31 85 mm gun. Although the gun could be made to fit, the turret interior was really too small to support the proper function of such a large weapon. The KV-1S-85 prototype is still preserved at the Kubinka armour museum outside Moscow.

armouring of the KV without commensurate improvements in engine power diminished its effective cross-country speed so much that it could not keep up with the fleet T-34s and T-60 light tanks. While the KV had been universally popular in 1941 and early 1942 because of its superior armour, by 1942 the Germans were introducing new guns and ammunition to deal with it. In June 1942, for example, Lt.Col. Strogiy, who commanded a tank brigade fighting on the Kerch peninsula, reported to STAVKA that his KVs had been penetrated by a new German round using the shaped-charge (HEAT) principle. This was a critical development since it meant that new ammunition could be developed for nearly any German artillery piece so as to penetrate the KV. Furthermore, it was the first step in the development of effective infantry anti-tank weapons such as the *panzerfaust* and *panzershreck*, which would begin to enter service by 1943. In addition, the Germans were deploying the new PAK 40 towed 75 mm anti-tank gun, and rearmed the PzKpfw

The KV-1S represented a major redesign of the KV. The new cast turret was considerably smaller than previous cast turrets and is easily distinguished by the use of a low commander's cupola. The hull has been redesigned and the rear engine deck slopes at a greater angle than previous types. New light weight wheels were also introduced in at least two variations. (Author)

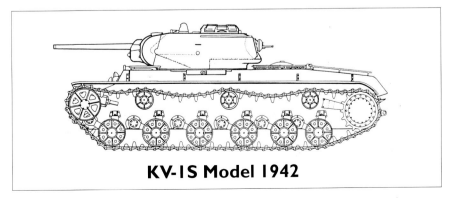

KV-1S Model 1942

KV Tank Production in World War II

(Production by quarter)

Year	1940	1941				1942				1943			
Quarter	I-IV	I	II	II	IV	I	II	III	IV	I	II	III	
Total	244	307	321	311	419	542	602	703	718	452	-	130	4,749

(Production vs. Losses)

Year	1940	1941	1942	1943
KV Production	244	1,358	2,565	582
KV Losses* –		900	1,200	1,300
Effective KV strength*	244	600	2,000	1,600

Loss and strength figures are rounded off; strength is at end of year. Combat data comes from: Gen.Col. G.F. Krivosheyev, Grif sekretnosti snyat: poteri Vooruzhennikh sil SSSR v voinakh, boevikh deistviyakh i voennikh konfliktakh, Statisicheskoye issledovaniye. (Voenizdat: 1993).

IV with a new long-barrelled 75 mm gun. One of the KV designers later candidly wrote about the situation: 'In 1942, there was still a lack of sufficient numbers of reliable heavy tanks in the Red Army to prevent the catastrophes in the Crimea and in the Kharkov area. The KV-1 had completely discredited itself, and with that shame came the discrediting of the concept of heavy tanks as well.'

Several of the top Soviet tank commanders were questioned about their views on Soviet armoured equipment by STAVKA. Gen. Pavel Rotmistrov, who began the war as a colonel commanding the 8th Tank Bde. and ended it in charge of the Soviet armoured forces, replied bluntly: 'The difficulty is that while there isn't much difference in speed between the light [T-60] and medium [T-34] on the roads, when moving cross-country the light tanks are quickly left behind. The heavy tank [KV] is already behind and often crushed local bridges which cut off units following behind. Under battlefield conditions, that too often meant that the T-34 alone arrived; the light tanks had difficulty fighting the German tanks anyway and the KVs were still delayed in the rear. It was also difficult to command these companies as they sometimes were equipped with different types of radios or none at all.' Rotmistrov argued that it would be more prudent to concentrate industrial resources on a single, 'universal' tank instead of the light, medium and heavy types.

To solve this problem, a two-track policy was adopted. Kotin and SKB-2 design bureaux were worried that the call for a single tank by influential officers like Rotmistrov would most likely lead to selection of the T-34 rather than the KV. A crash programme began on a KV with reduced armour called the KV-1S (S= *skorostnoi*, speedy), an attempt to decrease the disparity in automotive performance between the KV and the T-34. In April 1942, work also began on the KV-13, an attempt to develop a more compact version of the KV that retained its heavy armour while at the same time improving its automotive performance. It was hoped that the KV-13 would be a true universal tank, therefore bridging the gap between medium and heavy tanks.

New lightweight design

The KV-1S was an attempt to cut 5 tonnes of weight from the KV. One of the most important weight savings measures was the design of a much smaller turret. The hull returned to 75 mm side armour, from the 90 mm side armour of the KV-1 Model 1942. The rear of the hull was slightly modified by increasing the angle of the rear deck, saving additional weight. A new lightweight roadwheel was also introduced. To further improve automotive performance, the powertrain of the tank was completely upgraded, including a new clutch, new transmission and other improvements developed by N.F. Shashmurin. The combination of weight savings and powertrain improvements closed the gap in performance between the KV and the T-34, in part because the T-34 was becoming heavier and less nimble. One of the most important changes on the KV-1S was the redesign of the turret to take into account the lessons of tank fighting in 1941 and 1942. The commander was relieved of his responsibilities as loader, the redundant rear hull machine gunner being given this role instead. So the commander was moved from

The KV-14 was an assault gun version of the KV-1S, fitted with a 152 mm gun-howitzer in a fixed case-mate. When introduced into service in 1943, it was redesignated as SU-152. Here, the battery commander, Lt. F.N. Nagovitsyn gives instructions to the assault gun commander, Lt. S.F. Berezin, during operations on the 2nd Baltic Front in the late summer of 1944. (Soloviev)

the front right-side of the turret to the rear left-side, behind the gunner. In addition, the commander was given an all-round vision cupola to assist him in his main task of co-ordinating the action of the tank within the tank platoon and company, as well as acquiring enemy targets. One of the strange features of this vision cupola was that it lacked a hatch. The turret still had only a single hatch, mounted over the loader on the right side of the turret roof. The rear turret MG was moved from the centre to the left side, and could be operated if necessary by the commander. The prototype of the KV-1S carried 90 rounds of ammunition for the gun, but on the production vehicles this was increased to 114 rounds. The tank was designed so that it could be fitted with either the F-34 or ZIS-5 76.2 mm tank gun system, since by mid-1942, Chelyabinsk was producing both the T-34 and KV.

Trials of the prototype KV-1S were completed in the summer of 1942. However, staff studies conducted after the débâcle at Kiev led to more pressure to stan-dardise on a single tank. This was resisted by some army officials who still desired a heavily armoured tank to support the infantry. As a result, the mid-year tank programme ordered the Chelyabisnk tank plant to begin shifting a portion of its assembly lines from KV heavy tanks to T-34 tanks in August 1942. The KV-1S was accepted for production on 20 August 1942 and began to be built later in the month alongside T-34s.

New heavy tank formations

At a meeting with Stalin in September 1942 Gen. M. E. Katukov, who had so successfully used the new KV and T-34 tanks in the defence of Moscow in October 1941, was asked of his opinion of the quality of Soviet tanks. He replied: 'The T-34 fulfills all our hopes and has proven itself in combat. But the KV heavy tank... the soldiers don't like it... It is very heavy and clumsy and not very agile. It surmounts obstacles with great difficulty. It often damages bridges and becomes involved in other accidents. More to the point, it is

The SU-152 is easily distin-guished from all other KV variants by its fixed super-structure, and large 152mm howitzer. A 203 mm version was also contemplated but did not enter production. The hull is derived from the KV-1S type.(Author)

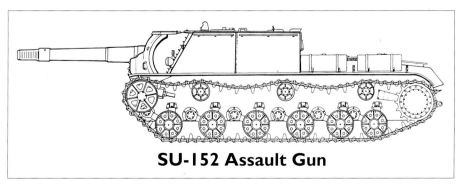

SU-152 Assault Gun

The SU-152 proved very successful; in 1943 it was one of the few armoured vehicles in the Red Army that could stop a Tiger or Panther, earning it the nickname Zvierboi ('Animal Hunter'). This is another view of the SU-152 of Lt. Berezin on the 2nd Baltic Front in 1944. By this time the improved ISU-152, on the new IS-2 Stalin chassis, was entering service. (Soloviev)

equipped with the same 76 mm gun as the T-34. This raises the question, to what extent is it superior to the T-34? If the KV had a more potent gun or one of greater calibre, then it might be possible to excuse its weight and other shortcomings.' After much debate, in October 1942 KVs were ordered removed from the mixed tank brigades and used instead to form separate heavy tank breakthrough regiments for use by army commanders in assault and infantry support missions.

Ironically, the KV-1S, the most nimble of the KV heavy tanks, arrived at a time when heavy armour rather than mobility would have been preferable. A total of 1,370 KV-1S were produced through April 1943 when KV production finally ended. Many KV-1S were delivered to regular tank brigades before the reorganisation took effect. Among the first units so equipped were those earmarked for the Stalingrad counter-offensive. The best-known of these was the 121st Tank Bde. of the 62nd Army, later granted the title 27th Guards Tank Bde. for its excellent performance in that campaign.

Universal tank

Parallel to work on the KV-1S, a SKB-2 design team

By 1943 the KV-1 had met its match with the arrival of the Tiger I and Panther. The thinner armour of the KV-1S could not resist the heavy firepower of the Tiger, and its own 76 mm gun was hopelessly inadequate against the thick armour of the new German tanks.

As a stop-gap measure, a small number of KV-85 tanks were manufactured until the new IS Stalin heavy tanks became available. This consisted of the turret originally intended for the new IS-1 Stalin heavy tank, mounted on a KV-1S hull modified with a set of fillets, widening its turret race.

headed by N. V. Tseits began work on the KV-13. Unlike the KV-1S, the KV-13 was in reality a whole new design. The ultimate objective of the programme was to develop a tank as well armoured as the KV but lighter and more maneuverable like the T-34. The KV-1 design was clearly too large to accomplish these goals, so the designers intended to create a smaller tank. One road wheel station was dropped compared to the standard KV, and dimensions were trimmed in most directions. The armour basis was 120 mm on the glacis, 75 mm on the hull sides, and 85 mm on the turret, roughly the level of the intial KV tanks. The armour was intended to be adequate to protect the tank against frontal attack by the German 88 mm gun. Internal volume was reduced, so that ammunition stowage fell to 65 rounds. The crew was reduced from five to three: the driver , loader, and the commander, who doubled as the gunner. A new powertrain was developed. Prototypes were built with both the KV track or the T-34 track.

The KV-13 design succeeded in reducing the weight to only 31 metric tons, compared to 42.5 for the KV-

1S and 47 for the basic KV-1. The road speed was also increased to 55 km/h (34 mph), compared to 43 km/h for the KV-1S and only 35 km/h for the KV-1. In June 1942, the T-34 design bureau at Nizhni Tagil joined the race with their own universal tank competitor, the T-43. This tank was patterned after the T-34, but had much heavier armour. Developments in Germany would soon make it clear that the universal tank concept had gone down the wrong path. Armour had been stressed over firepower, and the Germans would soon introduce new vehicles which would make the 76 mm guns on the KV-13 nearly useless. Furthermore, the success of the KV-1S led to the decision against producing the KV-13.

The German reaction - Tiger I

The Germans had not been idle after the heavy tank scare of 1941. Work was underway on two new tanks, the Panther medium tank, intended as an antidote to the T-34, and the Tiger I heavy tank intended as a response to the KV. The Tiger was the first of these ready, and a small number were deployed with

The KV-85 is easily distinguished through its use of the large 85mm gun turret, originally developed for the IS-1 heavy tank. In order to accomodate the larger turret ring diameter, there are tow fillets at the side which cover the enlarged ring. The hull of this vehicle is based on the KV-1S. (Author)

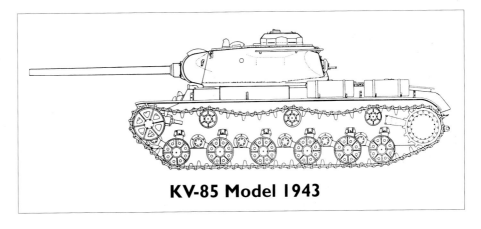

KV-85 Model 1943

Early testbeds for the IS Stalin series were built using KV components. The IS-2 mated the KV-13 hull with the 122 mm howitzer turret of the KV-9; the designation IS-2 was later applied to the definitive production model of the IS series with the 122 mm D-25T gun. (Slava Shpakovskiy)

s.Pz.Abt. 502 on the Leningrad Front in September 1942. The Red Army knew very little about this new tank until mid January, when one was captured after one of its first major actions. The captured Tiger I was quickly rushed to the proving ground at Kubinka and subjected to minute inspection.

The Tiger came as a nasty shock. It had 100 mm frontal armour – much too thick to be penetrated by the 76 mm gun arming all Red Army medium and heavy tanks. Furthermore, its 88 mm gun was capable of destroying any existing Soviet tank. There was no consensus on how important the Tiger would be to the future of the German armoured force. It had only been encountered a few times around Leningrad, and some officers thought it might only be a prototype. One of the great mysteries of World War II Soviet tank design is why the Red Army did not insist on rearming the KV with a more effective main gun, such as the 85 mm F-30, that had already been tested in 1941. Indeed, Zhozef Kotin, the head of SKB-2, ruefully remarked that the Red Army already had a counterpart to the Tiger, the Obiekt 220, in the summer of 1941. It is possible that the Main Artillery Directorate (GAU) was unwilling to adopt a new tank gun calibre due to the effect it would have on logistics. This was hardly a unique situation. The US Army also encountered the Tiger I, in 1943, yet was unprepared as late as June 1944 to deal with the Panther and Tiger in Normandy. The Soviet response was equally half-hearted.

Two prototype assault guns were on the drawing board, the KV-12 armed with the massive 203 mm howitzer, and the KV-14 armed with a no less impressive 152 mm ML-20 gun-howitzer. The KV-12 design never progressed beyond paper studies so far as is known. The KV-14, on the other hand, was rushed

through development. Although it was intended primarily as an assault gun for infantry support missions, it was viewed as a possible antidote to the new German heavy tank. Work on KV-14 was completed in early February 1943. The recoil of the 152 mm ML-20 gun-howitzer was too great for a turreted mounting like the KV-2, so it was mounted in a fixed casemate, similar to the German StuG. III. It employed the chassis of the KV-1S tank, which was still in production at the time. On 14 February 1943, the State Defence Committee (GKO), approved the KV-14 for Red Army service. It later received the designation SU-152 (*Samokhodnaya Ustanovka* = self-propelled mount). Production of the first SU-152 began on 1 March 1943, gradually replacing the KV-1S on the production line at Chelyabinsk. A total of 704 were manufactured before production ended in the autumn of 1943. The first heavy assault gun regiments were forming in May 1943.

Kursk

The Kursk-Orel battles in the summer of 1943 marked the swansong of the KVs; of 3,400 Soviet tanks on the Central Front, only 205 were 'heavies', and of these at least one regiment were Lend-Lease Churchills. Production of the KV-1S ended in April 1943 in favour of the T-34. The real problem was that the heavy tank had failed to keep pace with German developments, especially in tank guns. At Kursk, the KV-1S was woefully unprepared to deal with the new Panther and Tiger tanks. Both of these German tanks could penetrate the KV, but the KV was nearly powerless to defeat either type except at suicidally close ranges. The experience of the 2nd Bn., 181st Tank Bde., 18th Tank Corps near Petrovka illustrates the changed fortunes of the KV. Capt. P. Skrypin's battalion attacked a panzer unit in hilly terrain, but was badly torn up by the longer-range guns of the static Tigers. Ordering his KV-1S forward on an evasive course in a successful attempt to rally his shaken unit, Skrypin hit one Tiger at least three times, but without knocking it out. His KV was then hit twice, killing the loader and badly wounding Skrypin, who was dragged from the smouldering wreck by the driver and operator while the gunner remained at his post. The 76.2 mm gun was unable to cripple an approaching Tiger, and the gunner died from a third 88 mm hit. To protect Skrypin where he lay wounded in a shell hole, the driver returned to the burning KV and rammed the Tiger, whereupon the ammunition stowage exploded with shattering effect on both tanks.

The SU-152 fared better at Kursk. The first heavy assault gun regiment with 12 SU-152 – later raised to its full strength of 21 – was committed by High Command Reserve; in three weeks of combat it claimed 12 Tigers and seven Elefants, giving rise to the SU-152's unofficial nickname of *Zvierboi* – Animal Hunter.

The embarrassing technical performance of Soviet tanks at Kursk was mitigated only by the fact that the Germans had so few new Panthers and Tigers. But Soviet tankers insisted that they needed a 'longer arm' to deal with the new enemy tanks. The Kursk battle also revived the heavy tank idea. With the Tigers starting to appear in large numbers, the decision was made to revive heavy tank production. A new programme was begun, the IS Stalin heavy tank. (See New Vanguard 7: IS-2 Stalin). The IS series was in fact a continuation of the KV series, but the name change was felt prudent as Marshal Klimenti Voroshilov had fallen out of favour since the war began. The IS Stalin tank was an elaboration of the failed KV-13. It used many of the new components developed for the KV-13 such as the hull design, but returned to a full sized heavy tank capable of carrying a much larger gun.

Until the new IS tank was ready, it was decided to adapt a new tank gun to the existing KV-1S to provide some short-term capability. In August, the SKB-2 began work on two parallel projects. The Dukhov team began trials to see if a new 85 mm tank gun could be fit in the KV-1S without significant alteration. Although at least one prototype was completed, it quickly became evident that the turret was simply too small for such a weapon. Instead, a second team adapted the new turret developed for the IS heavy tank on to the KV-1S hull. This was accomplished by increasing the diameter of its turret ring by adding a pair of fillets to either hull side. The new turret was

In 1941, the Kotin design bureau developed an electronic mine clearing vehicle on the KV-2 chassis called the Obiekt 222; it never entered service. In 1944, some KV-1s, like this KV-1 Model 1941 with up-armoured welded turret, were fitted with the PT-34 mine trawl originally intended for the T-34 tank. This KV-1 mine roller tank was commanded by Jr.Lt. Lomovitskiy, and was used on the Karelian Front in June 1944 to break through Finnish minefields. (Suchatov)

armed with the D-5T 85 mm gun and the tank could accommodate 70 rounds of ammunition. On the original version of the tank, the hull MG station was retained. But once production began in September 1943, the later batches dispensed with the hull MG since the radio had been moved into the turret nearer to the commander, and this crewman dropped from the roster. A total of 130 KV-85s were produced in September-October 1943 before the assembly lines began shifting over to the IS Stalin heavy tank. The new turret raised the weight back up to 46 tons, posing the same automotive limitations as on earlier variants. The KV-85 was first committed to combat in the late autumn and early winter of 1943. Like the KV-1S, it served in dwindling numbers through the 1944 campaigns, but was quickly overshadowed by the superior IS Stalin series. At least one prototype was completed of a KV-85 armed with a 122 mm D-25T tank gun as the KV-122, but with IS production underway and so few KV-85s produced, there was little pressure to up-arm these vehicles.

THE PLATES

Plate A1: *KV-1 (appliqué), Tank Brigade, September 1941*

This tank brigade was partly equipped with KV-1E heavy tanks in the autumn of 1941 that had large patri-

Some old KV hulls continued in service right through the to end of the war. With its turret removed, this KV-1 Model 1940 is being used as an armoured recovery vehicle to tow a disabled T-34-85 in the wreckage of Berlin in

otic slogans chalked on the turret sides for propaganda purposes. This particular tank was labelled *Bey fashistkuyu gabinu!* – 'Crush the Fascist Vipers!'.

Plate A2: *KV-1 Model 1941 (up-armoured turret), 12th Tank Regiment, 1st Moscow Motor Rifle Division, August 1942*

This particular tank was commanded by Lt. Pavel Khoroshilov and was named *Bezposhadniy* ('Merciless'). It was paid for by contributions from Moscow artists who had won the Stalin prize. During the presentation ceremony, it was colourfully marked and sported a large cartoon of a Soviet tank firing on Hitler. The script below the tank is a list of the poets (right column) and painters (left column).

ТАНК ПОСТРОЕИ НА СРЕДСТВА ЛАУРЕАТОВ СТАЛИНСКИЙ ПРЕМИНИ

ПОЕТОВ	ХУДОЖИНКОВ
П. ГУСЕБА	КУКРЬІИНСКЬІ
С. МАРШАКА	М.КУПРЯНОВА
С. МИХАЛКОВА	П.КРЬІЛОВА
Н. ТИХОНОВА	Н. СОКОЛОВА

The script towards the front of the turret is a poem written for the occasion which reads:

Storming through the fire goes
ЩТЧРМОВОЙ ОГОНЪ ВЕЦЙ
Our KV heavy tank
НАЩ ПТЯЖЕПЬІЙ ТАНКИ
From the heartland it rolls
В ТЪІЛІ ФАШИСТУ ЗАХОЦИ
To smash the Nazi flank
БЕИ ЕГО ВО ФЛАНГ

Your fearless crew
ЕКИПА Ж БЕССТРА
Never rests
НЕ СМЬІКАЯ ГЛАЗ
As they fire in combat
Вь ІПОЛНЯЕТ БОЕВОЙ
Under Stalin's commands
СТАЛИНСКИЙ ПРИКАЗ

During combat from 1942 through the winter of 1943-44, this tank was credited with 12 German tanks, four SP guns, seven armoured vehicles, three guns, seven mortars, four heavy MGs, ten trucks, five motorcycles, a staff bus and a supply bus. These victory claims were recorded on the turret with rows of small geometric shapes.

Plate B1: *KV-1 Model 1940, German Pz.Regt. 1, winter 1941-42*

During the winter of 1941-42, some German units impressed captured Red Army tanks into service. In this case, the 1st Panzer Regiment has modified it by replacing the normal hatch with a German medium tank commander's cupola. The tank was repainted in panzer grey originally, but later whitewashed, leaving the Balkankreuz and tactical number on a small patch of the original colour.

Plate B2: *KV-1 Model 1942, Pz. Rgt. 22, 22nd Panzer Division, 1943*

In 1943, the German 22nd Panzer Division put several modified KV-1 tanks into service. The standard 76.2 mm gun was replaced by a German 7.5 cm L/43 Kanone from a PzKpfw IV tank. A German tank commander's cupola has been added to the roof. However, unlike the other KV shown here, the German cupola was not added over the normal hatch, but further forward on the right turret side, where a new hole was cut. These tanks were finished in the standard RAL 7028 dark yellow, with prominent Balkankreuz to avoid misidentification by friendly forces.

Plate C: *KV-1 Model 1942, 3/1 Tank Brigade, Finnish 1st Armoured Division, Ihantala, August 1944*

The Finnish Army captured and refurbished a few KV

tanks during the 1941-44 Continuation War. Most notably, the fenders of the vehicle have been rebuilt. The tank was painted in a standard Finnish scheme of dark green, with a pattern of medium grey and dark brown. The Finnish hakaristi insignia is black with a white shadow, and the tactical number is white.

Plate D: *KV-1 Model 1941, Soviet Heavy Tank Regiment, 1942*
The KV-1 Model 1941 (cast turret) weighed about 47 tons. The KV-1 Model 1941 was constructed in mixed fashion, with the hull and portions of the turret made from welded, homogenous rolled armour plate and the turret from a large homogenous armour casting. The turret armour varied by location: 90 mm mantlet, 82 mm face, 100 mm sides, 97 mm rear and 30 mm top. The hull was 75 mm on the glacis, 70 mm on the lower bow, 75 mm on the side, 42 mm on the roof, and 32-40 mm on the belly.

Plate E: *KV-1S, 5th Separate Guards Zaporozhe Heavy Tank Regiment, Stalingrad, December 1942*
In the autumn of 1942, the 5th Guards Heavy Tank Regiment was given 21 new KV-1S tanks, purchased with donations of 20 million roubles from the Glavsevmorput (GUSMP), the organisation responsible for Arctic sea voyages. These tanks were marked with the inscription *Sovyetskikh Polyarnik* ('Soviet Arctic Explorers'). The tanks were presented by Ivan D. Papanin, who had led the first drifting arctic station CP-1 in 1937-38 and who headed the GUSMP at the time. Later, the tank commanded by Guards sergeant K. Danilov (later, Lt. Smirnov), numbered '555', was renamed after I.D. Papanin as seen here.

The regiment was committed to the Stalingrad fighting in December 1942 near Kazachiy Kurgan, northwest of the city in support of the 65th Army of the Don Front. At the time, the tank was painted in a rough whitewash over the normal dark green finish, with the original markings remaining on large patches of green. The tactical number '555' was also painted on the rear of the turret as seen in the illustration. At Stalingrad, this tank was credited with knocking out two German tanks and 15 guns.

During a year of fighting through November 1943, the regiment was credited with knocking out 40 German tanks (including five Tigers), 53 SP guns, 142 other armoured vehicles, 138 anti-tank guns, 235 MGs and 124 bunkers. This particular tank was rebuilt in May 1944, and served with the 3rd Ukrainian Front during the Yassni-Kishniev battles in southern

A turretless KV-1 being used as a recovery vehicle tows a captured Tiger 1 heavy tank across Revolution Square in the Petrogradskiy section of Leningrad in 1944.

Ukraine. The tank later served with the 2nd Byelorussian Front and, towards the end of the war, was repainted in the markings seen in the front-view drawing. The 1945 scheme is overall dark green. The name I.D. Papanin is painted in a different style, with the symbols of two Hero of the Soviet Union red stars. The decorations painted on the turret front include the Order of the Red Banner, awarded to the Regiment on 23 February 1944, and to the left, the Order of Suvorov 3rd Class. Beneath these is the standard Guards insignia.

Plate F: *KV-8S Model 1943, Flamethrower Tank Regiment, summer 1944*
Flamethrower tanks were organised into separate units, intended to support offensive operations against German bunkers. This tank is painted in the standard style of markings for this period: a three digit white tactical number, while on the front of the turret is a white dedication marking *Trudovie Reservy Frontu* – 'Trade Reserves for the Front', recognising the organisation whose donations helped pay for the tank.

Plate G: *KV-1S, Heavy Tank Regiment, Battle of Berlin, April 1944*
Although the KV-1 had largely been replaced with IS-2 Stalin heavy tanks by the time of the 1945 offensive against Berlin, some were still in service. This particular vehicle was finished in the normal fashion: overall dark green with a two-digit white tactical number. The white turret identification band was intended to prevent attacks by Anglo-American fighter bombers as the two fronts closed in on Berlin. In some cases, the marking was elaborated with a large white cross over the roof of the tank.

Notes sur les planches en couleur

A1 KV-1 (appliqué), 1941. Cette brigade de chars était en partie équipée de chars lourds en automne 1941 qui portaient des slogans patriotiques inscrits en grosses lettres à la craie sur les côtés de la tourelle pour des raisons de propagande. Ce char spécifique portait le slogan 'Bey faashistkuyu gabinu!' ou 'Ecrasez les vipères fascistes !'. **A2 KV-1 Modèle 1941 (tourelle blindée).** Ce char spécifique était commandé par le Lt. Pavel Khoroshilov et baptisé Bezposhadniy ('Sans merci'). Il fut payé par les contributions d'artistes moscovites qui avaient remporté le prix Staline. Au cours de la cérémonie de présentation, il fut décoré avec beaucoup de couleurs et portait un grand dessin humoristique représentant un char soviétique tirant sur Hitler.

B1 KV-1 Modèle 1941. Au cours de l'hiver 1941-42, certaines unités allemandes mirent en service des chars de l'Armée Rouge qu'elles avaient capturés. Dans ce cas, le 1er Régiment Panzer l'a modifié en remplaçant la trappe normale par une coupole allemande de commandant pour chars de taille moyenne. Ce char fut tout d'abord repeint en gris panzer puis blanchi à la chaux par la suite, laissant les numéros Balkankreuz et tactique sur un petit morceau de la couleur d'origine. **B2 KV-1 Modèle 1942** En 1943, la 22ème Division Panzer allemande mit en service plusieurs chars KV-1 modifiés. Le canon standard 76,2mm fut remplacé par un Kanone allemand 7,5 cm L/43 provenant d'un char PzKpfw IV. Une coupole de commandant de char allemand a été ajoutée sur le toit. Ces chars étaient finis dans le jaune foncé standard RAL 7028 avec u Balkankreuz bien en évidence pour éviter les malentendus avec les forces alliées.

C KV-1 Modèle 1942. L'armée finnoise captura et rénova quelques chars KV durant la guerre russo-finnoise de 1941-44. En particulier, on remarquera que les chasse-pierres du véhicule ont été reconstruits. Le char était peint dans des couleurs finnoises standard : vert foncé avec un motif gris moyen et marron foncé. L'insigne hakaristi finnois est noire avec une ombre blanche et le numéro tactique est blanc.

D KV-1 Modèle 1941. Le KV-1 Modèle 1941 (tourelle coulée) pesait environ 47 tonnes. Le KV-1 Modèle 1941 était construit de manière mixte, le corps et certaines parties de la tourelle étant réalisés en blindage laminé homogène soudé et la tourelle étant une pièce coulée blindée homogène. Le blindage de la tourelle dépendait de la position : mantelet de 90 mm, avant 82 mm, côtés 100 mm, arrière 97 mm et dessus 30 mm. La coque était de 75mm sur les parements, 70mm sur le nez avant, 75 mm sur les côtés, 42mm sur le toit et 32-40 mm sur le ventre.

E KV-1S, décembre 1942. En automne 1942, le 5ème Régiment Blindés de Gardes reçut 21 nouveaux chars KV-IS achetés grâce à des donations de 20 millions de roubles de la Glavsevmorput (GUSMP), l'organisation responsables des voyages sur la mer arctique. Ces chars portaient l'inscription Sovyetskikh Polyarnik ('Explorateurs Polaires Soviètiques'). Le numéro tactique '555' apparaissait également à l'arrière de la tourelle comme on le voit sur l'illustration et, vers la fin de la guerre, il fut repeint au nombre des marques que l'on voit sur le dessin de la vue frontale. Les couleurs de 1945 sont le vert foncé uni.

F KV-8S Modèle 1943. Les chars à lance-flamme étaient organisés en unités séparées, dont l'intention était de soutenir les opérations offensives contre les bunkers allemands. Les marques de ce char correspondent au style standard pour cette période : un numéro tactique de trois chiffres en blanc alors qu'à l'avant de la tourelle on trouve une dédicace en blanc Trudovie Reservy Frontu 'Réserves commerciales pour le front' qui identifiait l'organisation dont les donations aidèrent à financer ce char.

G KV-1S, avril 1994. Bien que le KV-1 ait été presque entièrement remplacé par des chars lourds IS-2 Stalin au moment de l'offensive contre Berlin en 1945, certains étaient encore en service. Ce véhicule spécifique était fini de la manière normale : vert foncé uni avec un numéro tactique blanc à deux chiffres. La bande d'identification blanche de la tourelle avait pour objectif d'éviter les attaques des bombardiers anglo-américains lorsque les deux fronts se refermèrent sur Berlin. Dans certains cas, les marques étaient complétées d'une grosse croix blanche sur le toit du char.

Farbtafeln

A1 KV-1 (appliziert), 1941. Diese Panzerbrigade wurde im Herbst 1941 teilweise mit schweren Panzern KV-1E ausgerüstet, auf deren Turmseiten für Propagandazwecke mit großen Kreidebuchstaben patriotische Parolen aufgetragen waren. Der abgebildete Panzer trug die Aufschrift "Bey fashistkuyu gabinu!" - "Vernichtet die Faschisten-Schlangen!".
A2: KV-1 Modell 1941 (gepanzerter Gefechtsturm)
Dieser Panzer unterstand dem Kommando von Lt. Pavel Khoroshilov und hieß "Bezposhadniy" ("Gnadenlos"). Er wurde durch Beiträge von Moskauer Künstlern finanziert, die den Stalin-Preis gewonnen hatten. Bei der Übergabefeier wurde er bunt bemalt und trug eine große Zeichnung eines sowjetischen Panzers, der auf Hitler feuert.

B1 KV-1 Modell 1941. Im Winter 1941/42 setzten einige deutsche Einheiten requirierte Panzer der Roten Armee ein. Im dargestellten Fall hatte das 1. Panzer-Regiment das Fahrzeug modifiziert, indem es die normale Luke durch den Kommando-Panzerturm eines deutschen mittelschweren Panzers ersetzte. Ursprünglich wurde der Panzer auf Panzergrau umgespritzt, doch wurde er später weiß gestrichen, wobei das Balkankreuz und die taktische Nummer auf einem kleinen Feld in der Originalfarbe stehen blieben. **B2 KV-1 Modell 1942** 1943 setzte die deutsche 22. Panzerdivision mehrere modifizierte KV-1-Panzer ein. Das standardmäßige 76,2 mm-Geschütz wurde durch eine deutsche 7,5 cm L/43 Kanone von einem PzKpfw IV ersetzt. Auf das Dach wurde ein deutscher Panzerkommandoturm aufgesetzt. Diese Panzer waren im üblichen dunkelgelb (RAL 7028) gespritzt, und das Balkankreuz war deutlich erkenntlich, um Verwechslungen seitens befreundeter Streitkräfte zu vermeiden.

C KV-1 Modell 1942. Die finnische Armee requirierte im Zuge des Verlängerungskrieges 1941-44 einige KV-Panzer und rüstete sie um. Besonders fallen die umgebauten Kotflügel des Fahrzeugs auf. Der Panzer war in der üblichen finnischen Farbgebung dunkelgrün gespritzt und hatte ein Muster in mittelgrau und dunkelbraun. Das finnische "Hakaristi"-Zeichen ist schwarz mit einem weißen Schatten, die taktische Nummer ist weiß.

D KV-1 Modell 1941. Der KV-1 Modell 1941 (Gußturm) wog etwa 47 Tonnen. Der KV-1 Modell 1941 entstand in der sogenannten Mischbauweise, wobei der Rumpf und Teile des Turm aus geschweißten, homogen gerollten Panzerplatten bestand und der Turm aus einem großen homogenen Panzergußstück. Die Panzerung am Turm war je nach Lage unterschiedlich dick: 90 mm an der Kanonenblende, 82 mm an der Frontseite, 100 mm an den Seiten, 97 mm am Heck und 30 mm auf dem Dach. Der Rumpf war an der Bugplatte 75 mm dick, 70 mm am unteren Bug, 75 mm an der Seite, 42 mm auf dem Dach und 32-40 mm auf der Unterseite.

E KV-1S, Dezember 1942. Im Herbst 1942 erhielt das 5th Guards Heavy Tank Regiment 21 neue KV-1S-Panzer, die mit Spenden in Höhe von 20 Millionen Rubeln der Glavsevmorput (GUSMP) gekauft worden waren, der Organisation, die für arktische Seefahrten zuständig war. Diese Panzer trugen die Aufschrift "Sovyetskikh Polyarnik" ("Sowjetische Arktikforscher"). Die taktische Nummer "555" war vor der Abbildung ersichtlich am Heck des Turms aufgetragen. Gegen Ende des Krieges wurde sie wie der Zeichnung mit Vorderansicht ersichtlich neu gezeichnet. Die 1945er Farbgebung ist einheitlich dunkelgrün.

F KV-8S Modell 1943. Flammenwerfer-Panzer wurden in separate Einheiten zusammengefaßt, die die Offensive gegen deutsche Bunker unterstützen sollten. Dieser Panzer weist die für diese Zeit üblichen Zeichen auf: eine dreistellige, weiße taktische Nummer, auf der Vorderseite des Turms steht in weißen Buchstaben die Widmung "Trudovle Reservy Frontu" - "Handelsreserven für die Front", in Anerkennung der Organisation, deren Spenden zur Finanzierung des Panzers beigetragen hatten.

G KV-1S, April 1944. Obwohl der KV-1 bis zum Zeitpunkt der Offensive gegen Berlin 1945 weitgehend mit schweren Panzern IS-2 Stalin ersetzt worden war, dienten einige der Fahrzeuge noch. Das abgebildete Fahrzeug weist die übliche Farbgebung auf: einheitlich dunkelgrün mit einer zweistelligen, weißen taktischen Nummer. Der weiße Erkennungsstreifen am Turm sollte Angriffe von englisch-amerikanischen Kampfbombern verhindern, als die beiden Fronten Berlin in die Zange nahmen. In einigen Fällen wurde das Zeichen durch ein großes weißes Kreuz auf dem Dach des Panzers ergänzt.